## ADVANCE PRAISE FOR
### *MAKING YOUR OWN LUCK*

"Fred Glass is wise, funny, and unsparingly honest. *Making Your Own Luck* is more than just the story of a scrappy kid prevailing after weaving through the obstacles of an unconventional upbringing. Glass's memoir forces us to confront the excuses we often make that hold us back from success in our careers and in our lives. While Glass is a person of remarkable accomplishment, he makes a compelling case that you don't have to be born remarkable to achieve great things. He asks us to embrace the idea that we can—and should—shape our own destinies. He wants each of us to walk away from this entertaining and inspiring book saying, 'Well, if he can do it, why can't I?'"

—Bart Peterson, former mayor of Indianapolis

"A winning combination of a coming-of-age tale, an honest spiritual memoir, and a how-to book on building teamwork, all presented with a true writer's flair."

—James Martin, SJ, *New York Times* best-selling
author of *The Jesuit Guide to (Almost) Everything*

"Fred's friendly leadership style belies the keen human insights he has gained along the way as a son of a tavern owner, a practicing lawyer, and an adviser to city, state, and national leaders. As commissioner of the Big Ten, I had a front-row seat to admire and collaborate with a man who listened and led IU athletics to success while treating all around him with dignity and respect. *Making Your Own Luck* is a great read that I highly recommend."

—Jim Delany, former commissioner of the
Big Ten Conference

# MAKING YOUR OWN LUCK

# MAKING YOUR OWN LUCK

*From a Skid Row Bar to Rebuilding*
*Indiana University Athletics*

# FRED GLASS

*Foreword by Mark Cuban*

*Indiana University Press*

This book is a publication of

Indiana University Press
Office of Scholarly Publishing
Herman B Wells Library 350
1320 East 10th Street
Bloomington, Indiana 47405 USA

iupress.org

Manufactured in the United States of America
Fourth printing 2022

Cataloging information is available from the Library of Congress.

ISBN 978-0-253-05946-8 (hardback)
ISBN 978-0-253-05945-1 (paperback)
ISBN 978-0-253-05940-6 (ebook)

*To Barbara, Katie, Joe, Connor, George, Tom, Emily, Betsy, Ellie, Anna Rose, Lucy, and Eli, plus all the family I haven't yet met, as well as those I will never meet.*

# CONTENTS

# *INTRODUCTION*

On Father's Day, 2018, my daughter, Katie, gave me what turned out to be one of the greatest gifts I have ever received. It was a one-year subscription to a service that emailed me weekly questions about my life, shared my answers with Katie, gave her the opportunity to comment on them, and then bound them all into beautiful books. She gave one each to me and her three brothers. The book was an unexpected, emotional, magical sharing for all of us. My son Connor told me that he cried when he read it. It also gave me the desire and confidence to heed my late mother's admonition: "Fred, you have to write a book someday!" This is that book.

I have been given the opportunity to do some really cool things in my life: serving a mayor, a governor, a senator, and even a president; helping to bring to my hometown a long-term relationship with the NFL Colts, a regular rotation of NCAA Final Fours, a massive convention center expansion, Lucas Oil Stadium, and a Super Bowl; and being the athletic director at my alma mater, Indiana University. I've had a number of advantages in preparing for these opportunities, but I'm still just a knucklehead who grew up in a skid row bar, had an alcoholic father, struggled with anxieties and self-doubt, did a lot of goofy stuff, and made my share of stupid mistakes. I hope my odyssey serves as an example that it is ordinary people who do the kinds of things I've had the opportunity to do. I'm reminded of the words of legendary Pittsburgh Steelers coach Chuck Noll that I heard his former player Tony Dungy quote to the Colts as he coached them at a practice preparing for Super Bowl XLI: "Champions are champions not because they do anything extraordinary but because they do the ordinary things better than anyone else." The key is not being cowed from seizing opportunities by a feeling that we are not ready, or capable, or deserving, but rather taking ownership of them by believing in ourselves and making our own luck.

You know how some people just seem to be lucky? A lawyer sits next to a stranger on a plane, and by the time they land, she's won him over as a client. A coworker is selected by his boss for a choice career-enhancing assignment. People who are reluctant to seize opportunities can be quick to dismiss such results as mere happenstance, perhaps defining it as luck, blind luck. Doing so releases them from any responsibility for achieving similar results. Such folks seem to prefer sitting back to see what the world does for or to them over actually trying to be active players in their destinies.

I have become a believer in the maxim that "luck is what happens when preparation meets opportunity," most often attributed to the ancient Roman philosopher Seneca the Younger. The reason that lawyer was lucky may well have been because she made the effort to chat up her seatmate and was ready to effectively make the case for herself when she saw that he could be a potential client. The reason the coworker was lucky may well have been because he knew such an assignment was coming, and he made sure his boss knew he was interested and capable, including by exceeding expectations on his previous assignments. To paraphrase Arnold Palmer, the more I'm out pursuing opportunities, the luckier I get.

I have been very lucky, and much of it is the kind that Seneca describes. My preparation has met opportunities to provide an interesting, exciting, and rewarding life. While that preparation included navigating a variety of challenges, it is important to acknowledge I also have had substantial wind at my back, such as being raised by two college-educated parents in a middle-class home, having the opportunity to go to a Jesuit prep school, and not being subjected to racial discrimination. These and most other aspects of my preparation, such as the examples of my role models and other experiences thrust into my life, I neither generated, earned, nor sometimes even wanted. Still, my preparation has made me who I am and has given me a head start on making me a lucky man. I learned that some of the preparation I viewed at the time as being quite negative, most significantly growing up in the back of a skid row bar and my father's alcoholism, has ultimately had a very positive impact on my formation as a person and a leader.

The first section of this book describes the preparation, broadly defined, that has enabled me to recognize and seize a variety of opportunities. The second section of this book tells some of the stories of those opportunities and how, combined with my preparation, they have made me a lucky man. I respectfully suggest that by recognizing and seizing opportunities, I helped to make my own luck. I didn't set out to do that. I wasn't following a manual or a plan. I sort of intuitively stumbled on what has now become a series of precepts for pursuing and taking advantage of opportunities to "make your own luck." I hope that by clearly setting those precepts out here, I can spare you the challenges of discovering them on your own. They will be repeated throughout the stories in this book so that you can see how they have impacted my life so far. By utilizing these precepts to make your own luck, I believe ordinary folks like us can have a greater impact than we ever thought possible on our ability to do extraordinary things.

## Making Your Own Luck

1. Opportunities often come at inconvenient times. Don't let that prevent you from seizing them. Find a way.
2. Our greatest disappointments can create our greatest opportunities if we don't let them deter us.
3. Accept opportunities presented to you even if you're not sure you are ready, or even capable, because all that matters is that the person offering you the opportunity obviously believes you are.
4. Seize every opportunity to the fullest. Own it. Exceed expectations. Confirm the confidence that has been placed in you and show that you are capable of even more.
5. When choosing among opportunities, always choose the one that will open the most additional opportunities in the future.
6. Choose what you judge to be better opportunities over higher salaries.
7. Always do the right thing, even when no one knows or appreciates that you are and even when the right thing looks to some like the wrong thing.
8. Prepare intensely and methodically, but when the moment to perform comes, trust your preparation and just let go.
9. You don't have to feel your best to do your best. Don't build in excuses to fail. Succeed even in the face of perceived adversities.
10. When you go out, go out the right way.

Ironically perhaps, I found myself leaning on these touchstones as I rode the highs and lows of working on this book. In any event, you will see primarily in the second section of this book how these precepts of making your own luck positively impacted opportunities in my life, but first we turn to how I was prepared for them in the first place.

# MAKING YOUR OWN LUCK

# PREPARATION

# 1. EARLY LIFE IN A SKID ROW BAR

Mom cried on the way home. I'm not sure why, other than maybe she had a premonition of how hard it would be on her and our family for Dad to own the skid row bar for which he had just signed the final paperwork. It may also have been her seeing the previous owner's hand, as he likewise signed the paperwork, missing a few digits and wondering perhaps if Dad might face some similar fate. Mom and I had been sitting in one of the wooden booths of the bar, with its deep-red paint chipping off, watching Dad and the previous owner close the deal. My five-year-old hands were folded and resting on the linoleum tabletop. It was cold. The stale air smelled like smoke and somehow felt dirty. The tavern was closed, and although it was night, the inside lights were all off other than the buzzing, flickering red and green neon lights promoting "Bar/Liquors" and "Good Food." The bar was subtly illuminated by the streetlights shining in through the huge, grimy plate-glass window facing East Washington Street on Indianapolis's skid row.

I don't know why Dad suddenly wanted to own a bar. Maybe he wanted to be his own boss. As we'll see later, maybe it was just in his blood, his destiny. Even as a little kid, I sensed that he bridled working for the man. Insurance companies. The state attorney general's office. In any event, as hard as it was, and as much as I hated it being part of my life at the time, nothing has ultimately had as positive an impact on me as literally and figuratively growing up in the back of that skid row bar, which Dad named George's Liberty Bar. He liked to say, "Give me Liberty, or give me death!"

The Liberty was full of characters. They were folks most people would just walk past, avoiding eye contact, categorizing them as bums, winos, or vagrants. The gift to me was that I got to know them as individuals, as real people. I felt particularly close to Don Williams, a tough guy Dad often had doing work around the tavern and our home. Like pretty much all the tavern's clientele, he was a very hard drinker, but he also seemed to me more responsible and trustworthy than the rest. One time when I was about ten, Dad let Don take me a few blocks down Washington Street to the downtown Em-Roe Sporting Goods to buy some shoes I needed for basketball. When I was done, I found him and said, "Mr. Williams, I'm ready to go back to the bar if you are." I thought nothing of it, but he told Dad how proud he was that I had referred to him as Mr. Williams, and Dad in turn told me how proud he was of me that I had treated Mr. Williams with appropriate respect. That stuck with me: the impact you can have on people just by doing the right thing and treating them with respect, especially people who may not be used to it or expecting it, as well as the impact a parent can have on a child by praising them for behavior they would like to see replicated. It may be an old saw, but Dad was the first person to tell me that the true measure of a man is how he treats someone who can do him absolutely no good.

One of the great characters at the Liberty I knew only as "Tiger." He managed the Catholic Salvage secondhand clothes store next door. He was massively overweight and usually dressed in audacious, tight-fitting clothes. Animal prints were a favorite. I didn't recognize it at the time, and it was never discussed, but looking back, I realize Tiger was flamboyantly gay. I would talk with him frequently, both in his store and in the bar. Once he shared a great insight with me. He said, "Fred, this bar is my living room. The jukebox is my stereo. The steam table is my kitchen. Your dad is my friend." I looked at the tavern's patrons differently after that.

Of course, there were many more. Herb, who would often fight with his wife after they had been drinking until, during one fight, she shot him dead outside the bar. Mom, ever the tolerant idealist, thought it was awful that Herb's wife got arrested for murder. "Herb wouldn't want that. He'd understand that she was just drunk, got mad, and shot him."

Glenda was a prostitute who turned tricks at the seedy Atlas Hotel next to Tiger's place. Dad would always say, "Poor people have poor ways," which I would remember when my friends were making fun of people with duct tape securing their broken taillights. Dad would remark how tough she was, providing for herself and her kids that way, including the night one of her customers expired from a heart attack on top of her in the act.

Jack Olvy seemed to me to be a very normal man, like one of Dad's old friends from growing up in Saint Joan of Arc parish. Jack always reminded me how thin the line could be between a mainstream life and life on skid row.

Other than Dad's alcoholism, nothing has affected who I am more than George's Liberty Bar, the characters I met there, and the tough side of life to which it exposed me. Although at the time I resented that my parents had, intentionally or not, made the Liberty such a central feature of my life, I am now immensely grateful for the lessons that place taught me about people Hubert Humphrey would have said were in the shadows of life.

* * *

Around the time I started high school, Dad sold the Liberty and bought the old Led and Joe's Uptown Tavern, which had always been one of his go-to haunts as a (very good) customer. It was near where Dad grew up on "his corner" at Forty-Second and College, next door to the Kennington American Legion Post. The clientele was very different from that of the Liberty, consisting of mostly younger blue-collar workingmen, older salesmen, business guys, and not a lot of women. Still, it had its share of characters as well.

There was Fast Eddie, a smooth-talking conman who always had some scam working. I remember that somehow he got himself signed up as a distributor for Lawn-Boy lawn mowers. He had dozens of them stored in a garage off the alley behind the tavern that he would sell at a discount from his usual spot at the end of Dad's bar to Uptown patrons and others. We got a nice new one for free—I assume in recognition of Dad's in-kind contribution of Eddie's overhead. There was Leon, a tough gentle giant; Slim, a tall, slender, Fu Manchu–mustachioed pool hustler; Al, an erudite Englishman who would often wax poetic and occasionally tend bar; and Monte Brown, who looked a little like Jackson Browne and often tended bar for Dad.

The Uptown was very close to the Indiana State Fairgrounds. Whenever I would complain about something not being fair, Dad would tell me the only "fair" was the Indiana State Fair at Thirty-Eighth and Fall Creek, which I, in turn, would often tell my own children. I loved it when the fair was in town the last two weeks of every summer, as the bar would be frequented by a fascinating collection of carnies who would win a lot of bar bets by sticking entire knitting needles up their noses and such.

Being a teenager at the Uptown was more fun than being a little kid at the Liberty: I was close enough to home that I could come and go, I could appreciate more of what was going on, and it was a more useful time of life to have access to alcohol. Most mornings, I would ride to the Uptown with Dad, sweep and mop out the bar, and then hitchhike the seven miles to my high school, Brebeuf Jesuit Preparatory School, where I would often sell to my fellow freshmen and sophomores the pints of cherry vodka I had liberated from the Uptown that morning. In addition to those daily cleanings, I would also work weekends at the Uptown as a short-order cook, grilling tenderloins and what the guys liked to call "Freddy Burgers."

One night when I was staying at the house of a friend, Brian Brase, we borrowed his sister Shondel's Mustang bicycle, with a wicker basket with fake daisies on it, and trailed each other to the fairly nearby Uptown. I snuck in the walk-in cooler and was getting ready to make my getaway with a stay-cold pack of Stroh's Bohemian when I got nabbed by bartender Monte. He asked me what the hell I thought I was doing. I told him, fairly honestly, and he looked at me and said simply, "Carry on." The Stroh's fit nicely in Shondel's basket on the way back.

In 1977, before my senior prom, four or five couples went to the Uptown for drinks after we had gone out to dinner. My parents hosted us there. Such were the times, at least with my family. We were ahead of our time with a sophomore designated driver. I must say, I was resplendent in my attempt to pull off a riverboat gambler look: top hat, bolero tie, gloves, and walking stick.

Dad would annually dye his silver hair and goatee green for St. Patrick's Day. As I look back on it now, it seems very cool, but at the time it mortified me. My freshman year at Brebeuf, there was a father-son breakfast shortly after St. Patrick's Day where IU football coach Lee Corso was the speaker. Dad's hair was still green, and I was sick with embarrassment. One of my classmates, Joe Boarini, who I didn't know at the time, asked me what the deal was with Dad's hair. When I told him, he said, "Wow! That's so cool!" It made me feel so much better, and I've always remembered that as an example of the incredible impact even a simple kind comment can have on someone.

One of the most fun parts of the Uptown era for me was its participation in the annual radio station WNAP Raft Race, which for several years was a huge cultural phenomenon in Indianapolis. Guys at the Uptown built and rowed a raft in the race. Dad was the "commodore," so identified by a special shirt the guys had made for him. They almost got arrested by the Butler University police when they were on a test run on the canal running through the Butler campus. It didn't help when Uptown patron John Smeehuyzen taunted them: "What are you going to do, lock us up in the cafeteria?" The night before the race, the guys even wrote a song on the back of a brown grocery bag, no less, sung to the tune of "Proud Mary." They called it the "Ballad of Big George and the Uptown Boys." They claim they would have won the race, but they kept getting flashed by women in a competing raft who were trying to throw them off their game.

When Dad sold the Uptown in 1978, the *Indianapolis News* did a profile of him in which he extolled the virtues of taverns. He was quoted as saying, "People don't have the right concept of taverns. The pub was where literary people hung out, where the great ideas of the day were exchanged. The Revolutionary War started in a tavern" (June 15, 1978).

* * *

Nothing, not even George's Liberty Bar, which is a fairly close second, has had a greater impact on who I am than my father's alcoholism. He was never physically or verbally abusive to me or, as best I know, Mom, but he came home very drunk almost every night. The few nights that he didn't were like a treat, like being unexpectedly let out of jail. I had a prioritized mantra that I would pray as I repeatedly paced the exact same route around the house and looked out particular windows for him in an almost nightly ritual: "Please, God, let him come home safe, soon, and sober." I knew the last one was a loser, but it was worth a shot. Looking back, I can see this was a classic attempt, as the child of an alcoholic, to control a situation completely out of my control.

To this day, I exhibit many of the classic characteristics of an adult child of an alcoholic. I know this because of a wonderful 1983 book by Dr. Janet Geringer Woititz called, appropriately enough, *Adult Children of Alcoholics*, which was thankfully recommended to me by a fellow adult child of an alcoholic. It was an unexpected relief to better understand why I am the way I am and that it is "a thing." I highly recommend it to anyone who is similarly situated or loves someone who is similarly situated. Dr. Woititz's early summary of the thirteen characteristics of adult children of alcoholics gave me great insight into where some of my more challenging personality traits came from and, later in the book, how to deal with them. Several characteristics from her list clearly have applied to me in my life, especially when I was younger, including that adult children of alcoholics guess at what normal behavior is; have difficulty following a project through from beginning to end; judge themselves without mercy; take themselves very seriously; overreact to changes over which they have no control; constantly seek approval and affirmation; usually feel that they are different from other people; are super responsible or super irresponsible (I've been both!); and are extremely loyal, even in the face of evidence that the loyalty is undeserved (Woititz 1983, xviii–xix).

Not a very flattering list.

While I was pacing around praying, Mom would turn to the "taverns" page of her phonebook where she had listed the names and numbers of

Dad's twelve or so haunts and start calling them to see if he was there. Sometimes she'd talk to him. Sometimes I'm pretty sure he told the bartender to say he was not there. Sometimes the call might get him to come home. Most times it didn't. Once when she called him, he asked her if there was anything he could pick up for her on the way home. Mom said, "Yeah, one foot after the other." Dad thought this was so funny he had three or four more drinks laughing about it with his buddies before he came home. Sometimes the bartender, on condition of anonymity, would do the calling—to Mom—to rat out where Dad was so she would come and get him, usually because he was belligerently drunk. Many nights, Mom would drive around with me in the car looking for his red pickup truck at all the bars. The Red Key Tavern, his favorite, was where these drives with Mom usually started. Sometimes still on rainy fall evenings, I get that feeling of driving around with her looking for Dad.

Dad never owned the Red Key, but he did make considerable investments in it over the years, one beer at a time. Ironically, it has become our family's go-to meeting place, maybe like Dad's vision of the tavern as he described in that *Indianapolis News* article. Barb and I often walk there together on dates or to meet friends. It's where we go before and after weddings, funerals, civic events, and the like. Our kids now go there with their friends. A treasured memory is going to the Red Key with Barbara and our sons Connor and George, who were visiting from their out-of-town homes, for beers and cheeseburgers with Mom over her last Christmas. She died the following September at the ripe old age of ninety.

When I was about ten, Dad got beat up, drunk, outside the Aristocrat Tavern on North College Avenue, when it was still in a bad neighborhood, Dad's old neighborhood. It was supposedly a dispute over how Dad had parked. I always assumed he had given the wrong guys a hard time. Dad was so embarrassed for me to see him beat up like that, he cried. The only other time I ever saw him cry was at his younger cousin and goddaughter's funeral after she killed herself. He helped his childhood buddy Ed Madden coach my St. Thomas fifth and sixth grade football team, and when he did show up for practice, he was often drunk. I remember during a fifth grade St. Thomas basketball game, while I was *in the game*, spending most of my time looking out the gym window to see if I could see his red pickup truck pull up, sure that he was drunk and would come in and embarrass me.

Once Dad organized a hog roast picnic for a bunch of regulars from the Uptown on some undeveloped property he owned along the White River in the Rocky Ripple neighborhood of Indianapolis. Everyone got really drunk, with Dad leading the parade. He kept talking about jumping in the river and going swimming, and his friends were egging him on to do so. I begged him not to, and finally one of them, Cathy, whom I always liked, came to my support and said, "George, I know you are a great swimmer, but you are so drunk you might just start giggling and forget how." Dad thought this was funny, and it deescalated the situation.

A little later, at the same picnic, Dad had been drunkenly telling a story, absentmindedly swinging a very sharp knife, which had been used to carve the hog, right in front of—and much too close to—Mom. Nothing happened, but that night when I was going to bed, I told her how scared that made me. I didn't usually share my worries with her. "What if he had stabbed you?" I asked her.

Without missing a beat, Mom said, "Someone would have driven me to the hospital, and they would have sewn me up!" I found that amazingly comforting. With Dad as an alcoholic, my life seemed a constant stream of anxious what-ifs. Mom quickly took this one off the table, and I would try to remember her response whenever I started to whip myself into another what-if frenzy. Still do.

When I was in the Boy Scouts in seventh grade, there was a "hike" at Culver Military Academy where all the dads went and drank and smoked and cooked out. Dad was excited to go, as many of the dads were his pals from his Joan of Arc days. I didn't want him to go because I thought he would get drunk and embarrass me. I had never confronted him about his drinking before, but I mustered up all my courage and told him I didn't want him to go and why. He was very hurt. He didn't go. I had hoped by him hearing from me how hard his drinking was on me that maybe he would stop, but he didn't. He couldn't.

Dad would constantly drive drunk. Because it was so common and not generally as taboo as it thankfully is now, I didn't even realize how dangerous that was. He had multiple DWIs. After one, when he was sober, I heard him telling Mom about his having to go to drunk driving school. I was about eight, and I asked him what that was. He said, "It's where they teach you how to drive when you're drunk." He may have been an alcoholic, but he was also pretty funny. When I was out with him, and he was drunk, usually in the car, I'd pray that other people would give him room, literally and figuratively, and let it pass if he did something wrong or bad or provocative. It took a lot of worrying and ritual for me to keep most of the bad things from happening! I try to think about that when somebody does something that I feel somehow deserves my retribution. Maybe he or she has a kid praying that I will let it pass. Everybody is dealing with something. I wish I was better at remembering that.

It's funny. I never really thought of Dad as an alcoholic, although I always knew that he drank too much. The first time I ever connected that word to him was shortly after he was diagnosed with colon cancer. Mom and I were alone driving someplace, and she said she wondered if the cancer may have been caused by his alcoholism. Sort of matter-of-fact like that. I asked her if she thought he was an alcoholic, and she said, "Don't you?" I didn't. Or hadn't. He didn't seem like the ones I had seen in the movies. It didn't seem to keep him from working. He didn't beat us or anything. But from that moment on, I knew and accepted that he was an alcoholic, which I think started helping me be more sympathetic to him.

I should have recognized earlier how badly he really needed alcohol, like the time he proudly showed me, with Mom looking on with approval, the makeshift flask he had made out of one of Mom's large perfume bottles to get him through a long day working at the polls. He particularly enjoyed showing me how the bottle had a tube that had the effect of holding back some of its contents. "Look," Dad said to Mom's amusement, "it has a reserve tank! Like a Volkswagen." I couldn't laugh. The realization of how he needed that made me sad and how my unintentionally obvious sadness made Dad sad made me even sadder.

Throughout my childhood, I had a secret nemesis. Many nights, while I was lying in bed craving to go to sleep before it started doing it, I would shake uncontrollably. The worst part of it was before it started doing it, when I would wish beyond wishing that tonight it wouldn't happen. Then inevitably, I would have the little twitch. Sometimes I could reel it back in for a while before the shaking would start in earnest. I was preoccupied and terrified about it, day and night. Not surprisingly, I had a very hard time going to sleep. I'd start worrying more and more about it doing it the closer it got to bedtime. Somehow, irrationally and inexplicably, the shaking would be triggered by near hallucinogenic thoughts of combining shapes, spaces, and relative sizes of things in a way that made me uncomfortable beyond description.

Even now in the retelling, I have a touch of the old, awful feelings. "It doing it" was for years a central feature of my life, yet I told no one about it. Not friends. Not my parents. No one. I was scared. Would they think I was crazy? I was embarrassed. What if someone found out on a sleepover? Looking back, especially now as a parent, I am amazed that I didn't tell Mom about this. I would be shocked and disappointed if something like this was happening to one of my kids and they didn't tell me. But it reminds me that you never really know what's going on with people, even your own children. In any event, it's pretty clear in retrospect that these were classic panic attacks, no doubt brought on by all the anxiety related to Dad's alcoholism. I think worrying has been my misguided and irrational attempt to exercise my need to control things. I had no sense of that then. It would have helped to know there might be a reason this was happening to me.

Worrying about "it doing it" was the central component of a vast array of worries I would have, including about what Dad was going to do, how Mom was going to react, whether there would be a nuclear war, and where people could live given the housing crisis (I remember thinking as a little kid, maybe in the grassy median of the highway—no one seemed to be using it), just to name a few. The fear of "it doing it" was always lurking in the back of my mind and came front and center leading up to going to bed and then trying to go to sleep. As I got later into high school, it started to become less frequent, although it didn't totally fade away until I was well into college. I'm not sure why. Even after that, I have still tended to be a first-class worrier. I semifacetiously say, "Don't tell me my worrying doesn't help; nothing I worry about ever happens." More recently, I've gotten better at understanding why I worry—to control things—and that worrying truly doesn't do anything about the future but rob you of joy and peace in the present. I've gotten better following the maxim "Don't bleed until you're shot."

In the 2019 movie *A Beautiful Day in the Neighborhood*, Tom Hanks as Fred Rogers tells the troubled journalist profiling him that his father's shortcomings helped to make him the good man that he had become and therefore that he should appreciate those shortcomings, not be tormented by them. That was a very freeing observation for me, given my complicated relationship with my own father, obviously before his death, but even after. Especially as I've grown older, I have appreciated his many wonderful qualities, which of course have impacted me in positive ways. At the same time, I had always resented his alcoholism, especially while I was living at home. As Fred Rogers suggested, I have evolved over the years to appreciate that my more positive qualities don't only come from the good part of growing up but also the bad and even the ugly. I forgave my father's foibles long ago, but I have now grown to be grateful for them.

\* \* \*

It turned out being a saloonkeeper was in Dad's blood and was perhaps his destiny, maybe along with his cantankerous but giving nature, political and community engagement, and potentially even some mental health challenges that he may have been self-medicating to address.

My great-great-great-grandfather Valentin Glass and his wife, Catharine, arrived in New York from Bavaria, Germany, in 1851, with their sons, Jacob and George. They were leaving a Germany in turmoil after the failure of the German revolution, which had pursued liberal ideals such as German unification, a more democratic government, and human rights guarantees. They were among the thousands of revolutionaries who, voluntarily or involuntarily, left Germany during this time dissatisfied with the failure of the revolution and the restoration of the German Confederation in 1850.

George, my great-great-grandfather, ended up running a saloon in Madison, Indiana. I am his namesake, along with my grandfather, father, and son, all of whom have the first name George. His saloon advertised in the local paper: "Oysters served in every style on short notice. The choicest liquors and finest brands of cigars will always be found at the bar." In addition, George was frequently highlighted in local newspaper articles for his good deeds, such as adopting the infant daughter of "the late Mrs. Rust, the suicide," raising money to pay more than $100 in "liquor fines" owed by a local resident so he could be released from jail, calling out the theft of "a fine gold watch" by a pickpocket during a card game in his saloon and demanding its return, and the like. George's brother Frederick also owned a saloon just one storefront away from George's on Madison's Main Street, portending brother George and Bob Glass's saloons being near each other on Indianapolis's main street (Washington) about a century later.

In any event, Valentin's brood became prominent, if somewhat brash, citizens of Madison, who were all too often touched by tragedy. For example, Jacob was killed when he was a twenty-seven-year-old lieutenant colonel leading a charge of his all-German Union company during the Civil War Battle of Missionary Ridge. Three days earlier, he had presciently written his brother anticipating his "death in the next battle," exhorting him to erect a monument on his grave "of white marble, of considerable size and reflecting the occasion," and concluding, "So I bid you farewell and do not mourn my death as long as this Republic lives." I've always wondered whether Frederick gave a brotherly eye roll on the monument thing.

Still, I think Jacob's brother George, my great-great-grandfather, takes the family cake in the crazy story department. According to a contemporaneous newspaper article, at about half past ten o'clock on the night of November 4, 1880, in Madison, a crowd of boys were heard to yell for Jefferson Davis to raise "the ire of three very loyal citizens" across the street. "With the expressed intention of wreaking vengeance upon the boys, the three men . . . began wrangling with the boys. George Glass, who was standing near, remonstrated with the men, remarking that no attention should be paid to the yells, as the utterers were only boys. [One of the men] then turned upon Glass, and after a few words called him a 'd---d s-n of a b--h.' Glass immediately struck [him], and almost simultaneously with the delivery of the blow, Watson, who was standing a few feet away, opened fire upon him (Glass) with a pistol, firing two or three shots. Glass then drew a pistol and returned the fire. Watson continued firing, and his last shot passed through Glass's heart, killing him almost instantly."

Another newspaper article reported that "Dotsy Watson, the radical assassin, was heard to say before he murdered George Glass, that 'some doddamned Democrat would have to walk over his corpse or he would walk over theirs.'"

Watson was arrested and jailed. The first-quoted newspaper article went on to observe in the rather sensational style of the day that "members of the Republican party had employed Major Gordon, one of the ablest criminal lawyers in the country to defend the prisoner. A jury (God save the mark!) was set up, and the burlesque proceeded. . . . [They] brought in a verdict of 'not guilty'; the murderer was forthwith released, the curtain was rung down, and the judicial farce came to an end."

Yet another newspaper account concluded that Watson was acquitted by "a jury all the members of which were Republicans" who "thought it no particular harm for a Republican to shoot down a Democrat on the street."

Wow. You can't make this stuff up.

Dad's mother clearly had mental health issues. Dad remembered his father telling him and his brother Bob when he had to go on the road for work as an electrician (IBEW Local 481), "You boys are on your own, but I've hidden all the knives." He also remembered "visiting" her at the local insane asylum, Central State Hospital, by talking to her through a basement window with bars across it. Mom told me that when Dad would return home from dates with her, his mother would have covered his bed with religious pamphlets. No wonder he had so many demons.

## 2. JUST ANOTHER KNUCKLEHEAD

When I was a kid, all I wanted—perhaps like most kids—was to be like the other kids because I felt—perhaps like most kids—that I wasn't. Like the inspiring and amazing writer Anne Lamott expressed in her landmark 1994 work, *Bird by Bird*: "All I ever wanted was to belong, to wear that hat of belonging" (Lamott 1994, xvii). Looking back though, I wouldn't trade my rather quirky childhood because, as Fred Rogers reminds us, that childhood—even with its pain—ultimately has driven the life I have lived. My own childhood seems like a study of contrasts, a simultaneous and paradoxical mix of the seemingly normal, yet oddly different: Norman Rockwell meets Holden Caulfield. In some ways, I had the quintessential middle-class upbringing, but at the very same time, especially when you factor in Dad's alcoholism and George's Liberty Bar, it was also what you might call rather unconventional.

Unlike all my middle-class friends and their families (at least as far as I could tell), we were always financially living on the edge. A broken water heater wasn't replaced for days until Dad could scrape some extra money together and get some bojack from the tavern to install it (properly, I remember hoping). Because we often couldn't pay our bills, our heating oil was only delivered COD, and our heat was shut off more than once when we couldn't pay for an oil delivery. Once, when we couldn't put together the money for a while, we spent several winter nights without any heat other than the gas burners Mom would keep lit on the stove and the kerosene space heater Dad put in the living room. In college, he proudly took me, Mom, and my friend Andy Lamberson to a nice restaurant in Bloomington and encouraged us to order anything we wanted. Andy ordered crab legs

I felt horrible for disappointing him. I had also disappointed Barbara, who had shown up at my empty apartment with a bunch of her girlfriends to go to a pregame kegger this new boy she had met was having. It's incredible that I was ever able to recover from this with her, but in fairness to me, I had a good excuse. I was in jail. After I got out, having been released on my own recognizance, I went to Benson's to apologize to Wally. He was not happy, but amazingly, he gave me my job back—limited to functions minors could legally do (restocking, cleaning, and the like), and I worked there the rest of my time in college.

Because of my arrest, the Bensons had a hearing before the Indiana Alcoholic Beverage Commission, the same one Barbara would later help lead for twelve years as its vice chair, for the possible revocation of their license. Dad, who had had experiences—all negative—interacting with the ABC as a tavern licensee, came with me to quite emotionally testify as to how I had been in taverns "since before he could see over the bar." Wally's son Bob brought in a stack of fake IDs similar to mine that the Bensons had confiscated from would-be underage purchases since my arrest. Finding the Bensons hadn't done anything wrong, the ABC took no action against their license, much to my relief.

While I was out on my own recognizance, before my court date, I ran into another little problem. I was at the Old Oaken Bucket game in Bloomington drinking beer at halftime in the parking lot when I felt nature's call. I discreetly (or so I thought) went behind some parked cars to relieve myself, and the next thing I knew I was being arrested by an Indiana University Police Department cadet. The charges: underage consumption of alcohol and indecent exposure. There went my legal career! I was devastated. Charging me with indecent exposure, I thought, was outrageous. I hadn't been in front of anybody, but still it looked awful, and I feared it could keep me out of law school. The illegal consumption charge was bad enough, but at least it was just a "status offense," that is, it was only illegal because of my (under) age. I wasn't charged with public intoxication, an offense regardless of your age. Back in jail I went, but no being released on my own recognizance this time. That was only for a first offense. I had to pay bail to get out, which I did with a rubber check since I had no money. I subsequently borrowed some and deposited it to cover the check, as I didn't think actually stiffing a bail bondsman was a good idea.

With a court date pending for my two arrests and my ambition for law school hanging in the balance, I thought I better get a lawyer. On the date of my hearing, he and I sat in the courtroom while every single case got called and handled, leaving us for last. First, Monroe County Judge

John Baker read the charges: "From your first arrest, underage possession of alcohol. From your second arrest, underage consumption of alcohol." I looked up at him. He said: "Oh, you were expecting another charge? Well, it went away over the weekend." I knew it was an inappropriate charge, and I was glad this obviously learned jurist agreed. (Andy Lamberson would later revel in telling people that my indecent exposure charge had been dismissed for insufficient evidence.)

My lawyer then started a rosy description of my strong academics and so forth, but Judge Baker signaled him to stop. "Counselor, we all knew goofs like him in college. They get an A in organic chemistry but can't tie their own shoes. Glass, here's the deal: I'm giving you ninety days in jail, but I'm suspending the sentence assuming you do forty hours of community service, at which point I will expunge your record. But if you get caught in Monroe County setting a foot in a bar or drinking before you are twenty-one, I'm going to mount you upside down on that wall, and there's nothing your lawyer is going to be able to do about it. Do you understand that?" I did.

Although I had one final little problem in this whole fiasco. In college, I was a master procrastinator; now I know as an adult child of an alcoholic, it wasn't my fault! Even though the stakes for getting my community service done could not have been higher, I put off doing it. In fact, I waited until one week before my deadline for having it done before I even started calling the list of agencies I had been given by my probation officer at which to seek to do my court-mandated service. I had naively thought I could do my forty hours of public service in a forty-hour workweek, but when I called the agencies, they basically laughed at the notion. Now I was really screwed and freaked out. Judge Baker was already mad. What would happen when he found out that I didn't get my forty hours done even though I had months to do it? My ninety-day jail sentence was suspended pending completion of the hours. Would I be going to jail? What about law school now? I shared my desperate situation and desperate feelings with Andy. While initially sympathetic, he fairly quickly left to go out to the bars. And then the miracle happened.

Andy ran into our mutual probation officer, who didn't seem to know, or at least care, that Andy was out drinking underage and breaking his own probation. Andy told him my sad story and asked if there was any way he could help me out. "Sure," he reportedly said, "I can authorize a ninety-day extension. Consider it done." And it was. Bullet dodged. I signed up immediately to do my community service at the Rose Hill Cemetery, owned by the city of Bloomington. My foreman mockingly called me "Poli-Sci" because that's how I described what I was majoring in. I mostly cut grass, but a few times I actually helped bury people. My fondest memories are of playing "big casino" in the gravediggers' shack with the lifers while the rain poured down outside. It felt kinda like being in a movie.

Oh yeah, one last part. Years later when I was on Governor Evan Bayh's staff, part of my role from time to time was to interview finalists for judicial appointments and make recommendations to the governor. You guessed it. Judge Baker was a finalist for an appointment to the Indiana Court of Appeals, and a little over a decade after I was appearing before him, now he was appearing before me. Of course I didn't say anything about our previous encounter, and of course he didn't remember me. He was very well qualified, and the practical way he had handled my matter only reinforced that with me. I recommended him to the governor. He was appointed, has served with great distinction, and is, as of this writing, the longest-serving member of the court. Once I left the governor's office, I told John the story, and he got a huge kick out of it. We have been very friendly acquaintances ever since and have supported each other on a number of projects. It can be a small, round world, and we should always treat it as such.

My aberrant childhood experiences, especially the ones I didn't like at the time—most notably Dad's alcoholism, but also growing up in his bars and rental properties, our financial struggles, feelings of not belonging, and even my battles with anxiety—I believe ironically led to one of my greatest strengths as a leader: a strong sense of empathy. While also probably somewhat inborn, I think it was honed by a lot of engagement with adults as an only child, exposure to the different and downtrodden growing up in the Liberty, and probably the survival instincts you develop as the child of an alcoholic, especially the only child. I am grateful that my experiences help me to relate well to people, including different kinds of people, and to be especially sensitive to and aware of their concerns and what they care about. It's a blessing that most importantly has enriched my life on a personal basis, but it has also helped me to be successful professionally.

# 3. BARBARA

My rather dogged and ultimately successful courtship of Barbara is an intimate example of making my own luck.

I literally and figuratively dreamed about meeting and marrying Barbara before I met her: a fun, smart, beautiful, brown-haired, brown-eyed woman who I loved and loved me back. I could see this woman in my dreams, and she looked just like Barbara. In real life, I met her at an IU football game my junior, her senior, year at IU. Our mutual friend Bobby Clifford introduced us. Shortly after we met, she was going to be the maid of honor in her younger sister's wedding, and Bobby was going to take her as a platonic favor to her. I shamelessly pushed Bobby out of the picture—"You don't even like her," I overstated—and served as her date, unfortunately, also rather platonically at this point in time.

I spent the reception schmoozing her family in an effort to triangulate her affection. Many of her relatives would tell Barbara that they liked her new boyfriend (me!), to which she would strongly reply, "He is *not* my boyfriend."

A couple of weeks later, I dropped by her apartment, where unbeknownst to me, her landlord was in the process of exploding a "bug bomb." With apparently nowhere else to go, she—more reluctantly than I would have liked—agreed to go out with me rather than stay back and breath in insecticide. We went to Skyline Chili, and I had a full "five-way," but she didn't want anything. Because I had exhausted my limited resources on the chili, I then had to borrow money from her to buy the twelve-pack of beer we had decided to get for watching TV back at my apartment. It can't be said that she didn't know what she was getting into with me. Perhaps amazingly, given my lack of chivalry on the beer-money-borrowing episode, we had an enjoyable evening on our official first date. It may never have happened if it hadn't been for that bug bomb. In retrospect, I see God's hand in that—what the Jesuits refer to as "God in all things." More on that and other Jesuit philosophies in the next chapter.

Barbara and I seemed to be doing well after that, but then rather abruptly she didn't seem real interested in me anymore. I checked with one of her roommates and her best friend from first grade, Patrice Sheehan, who rather casually told me, "Oh, Barbara doesn't like boys who like her." I didn't give up, but I did give her some room. That seemed to work, and before long we were spending more and more time together as the fall semester moved to its close.

If there was a moment that I fell in love with Barbara, it was at the very end of that year, on New Year's Eve 1979. It was after midnight, and we were in a cab on our way to my house to celebrate with my parents. Dad would even be home. He never went out on New Year's Eve. "Amateur Night," he called it. Barbara and I were sitting in the back of the cab together. "Brandy, You're a Fine Girl" came on the radio, and Barbara proceeded to lip-synch it to me with silly gusto. That was it. I was smitten.

From that time on, we were fairly inseparable through the spring semester. There were lots of parties, dinners at Nick's and the Porthole on Lake Lemon for catfish, running around in my roommate's Fiat convertible, and the like. We would often hang out with my roommates at my apartment at 1700 North Jackson (555 Lava Way) or with her roommates at her university apartment at Mason Hall (part of Willkie Quad), from which I would often appropriate rolls of their high-quality university-supplied toilet paper.

I subsequently started law school in Indianapolis the fall of 1981. During those tough economic times, most of the job opportunities were in Texas, and it probably made sense for Barbara to go there too. Although she never made it "either/or," I believed if she left at this point, we wouldn't stay together. That would just be the nature of things. I didn't want that, but I was only twenty-two, and pre-Barbara, Dad had told me not to get married until I was thirty. Still, I loved her and didn't want to lose her. We went to an IU football game with my parents. They knew what was coming, and Dad kept winking and smiling at Barbara, who didn't know what was about to happen and thought he was being weird. Given that we had met at an IU game, it also felt as if we were coming full circle. Afterward, she and I went to Brown County State Park and took a walk through the woods. We came upon a boulder and sat down on it. During a kiss, I took the ring box out of my pocket and put it in her hand. She pulled back and looked at me, and I asked her to marry me. I called it giving her "the rock on the rock." She said yes.

We were married the following spring, May 15, 1982, by Father Joe Casey, SJ, from Brebeuf in St. Andrew the Apostle Catholic Church, Barbara's home parish. My childhood friend Brian Brase was my best man, and Barbara's sister Diane was her maid of honor. Again, there was a certain symmetry in that Barbara had been Diane's maid of honor on our unofficial first "date."

Of course, the greatest of the many great things about marrying Barbara was having our four children, Katie, Joe, Connor, and George; welcoming Katie's husband, Tom, and Joe's wife, Emily; and cherishing our grandchildren, Betsy, Ellie, Anna Rose, Lucy, and Eli.

Marrying Barbara was the best decision I've ever made. I feel God blessed me with the confidence to keep after her even after she tried to shake me off and then to follow my heart and marry her even though we were so young. I have never once doubted her love for me, and I hope she has never doubted my love for her. What an amazing gift that is. I truly believe that being with her was my destiny. Opportunities often come at inconvenient times. Don't let that prevent you from seizing them. Find a way.

be with Joe and Lucy. They ended up not being able to come, but I stayed anyway. When it came time for the reading of the Gospel, it was as if it was speaking directly to me. It was the Gospel about "turning the other cheek" and following Jesus's prime directive to "love one another," even those—especially those—who hate you. Jesus points out that it is no great virtue to love those who love you, noting that even evil people love their own families. I felt as if God was speaking to me by bringing all these perspectives into my life when I particularly needed them. God in all things. Of course, I already knew this Gospel, but listening to it on that day in my then state of mind was like hearing it for the first time. I felt totally empowered. I suddenly realized I could love this person who was hating me and, in the process, take away all the power I was allowing his hatred to have over me. It was a transformational moment for me in which I truly applied a lesson I'd been hearing my whole life. I have no doubt that God brought me to that moment and gave me the grace to hear what that Gospel was trying to tell me. It may be obvious to find God in the Gospel, but like with finding God in anything, the key is being willing to see what God is trying to show you.

## 2. Men and Women for Others

When I was at Brebeuf, our motto was "Men for Others." This fundamental Jesuit value has appropriately since been expanded in most contexts to be "Men and Women for Others." In a closely related and very important concept, Ignatius says in his *Spiritual Exercises* that love needs to express itself in deeds more than words; thus, we are called to serve our neighbors. We can't, for example, declare ourselves saved by publicly declaring Jesus as our Lord and Savior and then turn our back on the needs of our neighbors and still reasonably expect God's favor. Although there are many aspects of traditional Catholic teachings that I find quite challenging, particularly as to women and the LGBTQ community, I have always been proud that Catholics believe it's not what you say, it's what you do. The Jesuits' express call for us to be men and women in service to others, combined with how that call was modeled by Dad and Mom, has been a powerful driver of my lifelong interest in servant leadership.

## 3. The Examen

The Examen is a daily prayer of reflection Ignatius set forth in his *Spiritual Exercises*. In short, it calls on us to give thanks for benefits of the day; recall the events of the day, remembering God is present to help us with our challenges; reflect on where we may have fallen short and are sorry; and ask for God's forgiveness and help in doing better tomorrow.

One of the beauties of the Examen is the depth it combines with its simplicity. At its essence, it is somewhat similar to the admonition of Ferris Bueller: "Life moves pretty fast. If you don't stop and look around once in a while, you could miss it." Okay, that's a bit of a stretch, but they both call on us to reflect on our daily lives in real time. When I practice the Examen, which I confess I don't as "religiously" as I should, it has the unexpected effect on me of making me more mindful of my day-to-day behavior—especially behavior of which I am not proud—because I know I'm going to have to face the music of revisiting that behavior tomorrow during my Examen.

### 4. The Magis

Father Martin describes the *magis* this way: the magis means doing the more, the greater, for God. When you work, give your all. When you make plans, plan boldly. And when you dream, dream big. But, as David Fleming recently wrote to me, the magis is comparative. The more, not the most. The greater, not the greatest. "Ignatius never works with superlatives," said Fleming. "When we want to do the best, we may get frozen. If we want to do what might be better, we are able to choose" (Martin 2010, 369). I love that particularly: "The more, not the most." Especially for procrastinators and perfectionists like me, it's a reminder that perfect is the enemy of good and a call not to let the inability to make things perfect keep us from making them better. Mother Teresa said it this way: "If you can't feed a hundred people, then feed just one." The magis has repeatedly inspired me to take on challenging works even though any particular effort in completing that work can seem insignificant and insufficient. By focusing on making things better, not necessarily the best, we can make progress on important works both big and small.

### 5. Cura Personalis

*Cura personalis*, Latin for "care for the whole person," has two distinct but complementary meanings. First, it calls us to ensure the fullest possible development of all the talents of each member of the community. Second, it calls us to respect all that makes up every individual, especially differences, and to recognize that individuals with differences from the main community are in a position to contribute particularly valuable perspectives for the rest of the community.

    *Cura personalis* was one of the most important concepts we utilized in rebuilding IU Athletics. We expressly and deliberately focused on caring for the whole person of our students: athletically, academically, *and* personally. Although we made substantial investments and realized substantial progress in all three areas, it was the third, personal development, where we really distinguished IU Athletics from its peers. *Cura personalis* is the inspiration and foundation of the central feature of the cultural and physical rebuild of IU Athletics: the Excellence Academy. Moreover, as *cura personalis* calls us to do, IU Athletics actively embraced diversity and inclusivity as one of its bedrock values.

## 6. THE PRESUPPOSITION

Ignatius's Presupposition, as described in *The Spiritual Exercises*, calls us "to be more eager to put a good interpretation on a neighbor's statement than to condemn it" (Martin 2010, 234). I like the way Father Martin puts it: "You approach every interaction with an open mind and heart by presuming—even when it's hard to do so—that the other person is doing his or her best and isn't out to get you" (Martin 2010, 235). As Father Martin notes, we tend to judge others by their actions, but *we* expect to be judged by our intentions. We also embraced the Presupposition as a bedrock value of IU Athletics and regularly discussed the importance and value of assuming those we interact with are coming to the interaction in good faith.

Father Martin also reminds us that we never know the problems people are dealing with, including those that may make them hard for us to deal with. This was brought home to me by the suicide of nineteen-year-old Zach Hollywood, a Ball State University basketball player who tweeted just before he killed himself: "Be careful what you say to everyone because you don't know what kind of battles they are going through."

## 7. CASUISTRY

Casuistry is a centuries-old method of moral reasoning, closely associated with the Jesuits, which calls on us to reason through problems on a case-by-case basis, "delving into the particulars" as opposed to deductive reasoning from general principles. Because casuistry often challenges well-established principles and the status quo, as Jesuits are wont to do, it is sometimes wrongly and pejoratively portrayed as excessively subtle reasoning intended to rationalize or mislead. Casuistry reminds us that facts matter and that fair isn't treating everything alike, but rather like things alike. Perhaps, without recognizing it, the concept of casuistry is why I have never believed in a zero-tolerance policy for anyone or anything in any of my roles because of the potential unintended consequences of deferring to an outcome purposefully blind to the underlying circumstances.

## 8. Reflection

Including, but beyond, the Examen, one of the most valuable Jesuit teachings for me has been their emphasis on the importance of reflection. My tendency is, once something has been experienced or accomplished, to quickly be on to the next thing. Among other things, the Ignatian premium on reflection has helped me to better savor experiences and celebrate accomplishments and by so doing lead a more fulfilling life.

## 9. Detachment

Detachment is the concept of being "indifferent" (Martin 2010, 306)—not unconcerned or unimportant, but rather impartial and unbiased: "The ability to be detached from one's initial biases and to step back, the willingness to carefully balance the alternatives" (Martin 2010, 306). I try to practice detachment in my decision-making by wringing the emotion and passion out of it and not being afraid of the outcome produced by detached analysis. In law school, a professor suggested we pretend in class and on exams that we were doing the work for a client, as opposed to ourselves, to take the pressure off us by creating what he called "distance," but what I think could fairly be called Ignatian "detachment." For years, before I knew detachment was a thing, I would apply my professor's advice to a host of real-life situations where I would pretend to be advising myself rather than acting myself, which I believe led to more balanced, less emotional decisions and better outcomes.

The leadership and life lessons the Jesuits taught me and the introduction to the genius of St. Ignatius and his teachings ultimately have had the most positive impact on my formation, setting aside the rather complicated and at least initially negative impact of Dad's alcoholism and the Liberty Bar. From a reluctant enrollee at Brebeuf, the Jesuits and their philosophies have grown to be a massive blessing in my life and those of my children. They have been instrumental in the peace and contentment I've been able to derive from my personal spiritual journey, as well as a crucial component of any success I've had as a leader, particularly as the athletic director at Indiana University, as you will see in chapter 13.

Another brief interaction with Dad has had a lasting impact on my approach in both politics and public service. It was the height of the Vietnam War, and LBJ was still president. I was probably eight years old. There was a front-page headline and a story in the *Indianapolis Star* criticizing Johnson's veracity in how he was prosecuting the war. This jarred me. He was the president of the United States! He wouldn't do something that was wrong! I asked Dad how that could be, and he said sometimes even presidents make mistakes. He went on to say sometimes the people around the president—even his supposed friends—tell the president what he wants to hear instead of what they really think because they are afraid of making the president mad and they won't be his friend anymore or allowed to be one of his advisors. I asked Dad why that was, and he told me that power does funny things to people.

I vividly remember vowing to myself then and there that if I ever had a chance to advise an officeholder, I would tell him the truth no matter the consequences to me. That clear-minded promise of an eight-year-old has stood me in good stead as I've dealt with such situations as an adult with more nuanced and complicated conditions than I understood to be at play back then with LBJ. The irony is that I have found that the more willing I am to "tell truth to power" to candidates, officeholders, colleagues, and clients, the more I become a trusted advisor, even if in the short run I feel more like a shot messenger.

In 1968, when I was in third grade, I was playing on the playground during recess at St. Thomas when I noticed a big hubbub going on. It seemed Robert Kennedy was on his way to Butler University to give a speech for his primary presidential campaign, saw the Catholic school kids in our uniforms out playing, and decided to stop and wade in with them. In one of my most memorable moments, political or otherwise, I got to shake Senator Kennedy's hand. Of course, within weeks he would be tragically assassinated in Los Angeles.

I have seen in person every Democratic president since I was born. My parents took me to see President Kennedy at the Indianapolis airport. People of a certain age remember where they were when they first heard President Kennedy was assassinated, and I am no exception even though I was only four years old. Mom was crying when she picked me up that day from Miss Cook's kindergarten, and after I asked her, she told me why. I remember in detail watching the coverage of JFK's funeral on our little black-and-white TV. The riderless horse. John-John's salute. Mom took me on my first bus ride to see President Johnson at an event on Monument Circle, and by so doing, she showed me that public policy, government, and politics were important and honorable. I saw and met President Carter at a Jefferson-Jackson Day Dinner in Indianapolis. My friend Brian Brase and I, still in high school, were asked by a politically active family friend to volunteer at the dinner. While not part of our real (boring) assignment to hand out campaign literature, we pretended to be secret service agents with fake earphone plugs, talking into phantom radios in our suit jacket sleeves and positioning ourselves quite near the podium where President Carter spoke. The guy who carried the presidential seal to hang on the lectern before the president spoke was actually asking me for instructions on how and when to do it! We were lucky not to be killed by an authentic counterpart. I was President Clinton's Indiana state chairman in 1996 and met him numerous times. I met President Obama at the White House with the national championship Indiana University men's soccer team.

Meeting and marrying my wife, Barbara, has also been a formative and critical part of my life, our lives, in government and politics. It is hard to overstate how important to our relationship is that we were both raised as strong Democrats and have carried those values through our lives: brought separately to our relationship but made stronger as we bound them together. Conversely, it is hard to overstate how important our mutual commitment to Democratic values has been to the strength of our overall relationship. In grade school, Barbara announced to her family that she could never marry a Republican. That's my girl! Her first campaign was when she was in grade school, working for one of her former St. Andrew's teachers, Dave Evans, in his longshot bid for congress—he won. When we met, it was a mutual passion for politics that gave us something to talk about. I was usually shy with girls, and this helped me feel immediately comfortable and confident with Barbara.

As a kid, I had always wanted to be the governor of Indiana—until after law school, when I saw how hard that kind of life was on people and their families. I found a great niche I loved working behind the scenes as a "staff guy." As I came of age, the local and state political landscape was so dominated by Republicans that I never thought there would be much real opportunity for me as a Democrat. But things have a way of changing. As I'll describe later in the book, my parents modeling servant leadership and the worthiness of politics and public service prepared me to pursue and seize those kind of opportunities later in my life.

Ironically perhaps, I've been strongly encouraged from time to time, especially when I was the AD at IU, to run for governor. Twelve-year-old Fred would be very disappointed to know that I haven't had any interest in that for decades. Still, government and politics have been a very rewarding part of my life, in a way differently—but ultimately better—than I imagined.

He asked me how old I was (twenty-four), and he said, "You'll practice law for forty or fifty years. Why are you in such a damn hurry?" Then he gave me maybe the single greatest piece of career advice I ever heard, as basic as it may sound: when choosing among opportunities, always choose the one that will open the most additional opportunities in the future.

Under that test, the clerkship was the clear choice. Back then, you could only get clerkships right out of law school, so if I didn't take it now, I would never get another opportunity to do so. On the other hand, Ice Miller hired bunches of lawyers every year, so there was a good chance I'd only be more attractive to them after the federal clerkship experience, and they might well offer me that job again. Barbara was generous and graceful in supporting me whichever job I chose, even when I chose the clerkship, which paid less than half of what Ice Miller was offering.

This was the first of many times—every time, come to think of it—when the job I chose paid significantly less than another option. Of course, I didn't do so because it paid less but because it was the better opportunity. I report this track record of taking the lowest-paid job available not to polish my halo and suggest that I don't care about money (I do), but rather to encourage you to select opportunities on the basis of which one you believe you would like best and provides the most upside, not that pays the most. If you do that, the money usually ultimately takes care of itself. Choose what you judge to be better opportunities over higher salaries.

I had a tremendous experience working for "kindly old Judge Dillin," as he would often refer to himself. He was a great writer with tight and pithy prose, and I learned much trying to emulate his style as I drafted his opinions. Elected to the General Assembly at twenty-three, he had close to five decades of political and governmental stories from which I learned much in his retelling. For example, he astutely and helpfully taught me that "there's two reasons for every law: the good one and the real one." I've applied that concept to more than legislation in my career. Judge Dillin called me "Save the World," in part because of his challenge with names, but also because of my inclination to take progressive positions and the side of the underdogs in the litigation before his court. He was a valued and giving mentor to me for the rest of his life.

While I was working for the judge, some of my law school buddies and I organized a team for the lawyer softball league. In looking for a sponsor for our team, I reached out to an old friend from college, Chris Hall, who was the manager of a downtown chili and beer joint called Charlie and Barney's. Chris seemed receptive to the idea, but then I never heard another thing from him. After a couple of weeks, I finally got in touch with him and asked him what was going on. Chris told me, "I called my boss and told him how great this was going to be, just like you described it, and he just said, 'Chris, is the chili hot? You worry about keeping the chili hot, and I'll worry about the other stuff.'" I was bummed we didn't get the sponsorship, but I loved the concept of "Chris, is the chili hot?" I've repeated those words and that story innumerable times in the ensuing nearly forty years as a reality check for myself and others. There are times to think big, but first you have to identify and focus on executing your primary function. Keep the chili hot.

As my clerkship drew to a close, I was fortunate that Ice Miller did again offer me a job, but again I made a different choice. I chose Callahan & Riley because I thought it was a better opportunity for me, getting in on the ground floor of a small but well-respected litigation firm. Barbara again was supportive even though it also paid significantly less than Ice Miller. I had a great experience there. Their philosophy was that I was not just a hired hand but a future partner. My writing continued to improve, especially under the hands-on tutelage of senior partner Bryce Bennett, an outstanding writer. Not insignificantly, although I had always been one of those messy desk guys who "knew where everything was," because of the expectation at Callahan & Riley to keep a clean desk, I did so, which dramatically improved my organization and productivity. But after a couple of years, Evan Bayh called, and I left for the governor's office and, of course, a big pay cut. Choose what you judge to be better opportunities over higher salaries.

Fig. 1. George's Liberty Bar at East and Washington Streets on Indianapolis's skid row. Courtesy of the author.

Fig. 2. Dad tending bar at the Liberty. Notice the JFK picture and quote hanging over the cigarette machine. Courtesy of the author.

Fig. 3. My Liberty buddy Don Williams (*left*) with two other regulars, Jim Gillium and Craig Mott. Courtesy of the author.

Fig. 4. Trying for that riverboat gambler look pre–senior prom at the Uptown with date and lifelong friend Linda Baker Hullett. Courtesy of the author.

Fig. 5. Dad with his green hair and beard on St. Patrick's Day at the Uptown with two regulars. Courtesy of the author.

Fig. 6. With Connor (*left*), George (*right*), and Mom during her last Christmas at our beloved Red Key Tavern. Courtesy of the author.

Fig. 7. Mom and Dad on their wedding day outside St. John the Baptist Catholic Church in Tipton, Indiana. Notice the cig in Dad's hand. Courtesy of the author.

Fig. 8. With my buddies Tommy (*middle*) and Jimmy (*right*) Galloway getting ready to play army. Courtesy of the author.

Fig. 9. Barbara and I cheesing in my roommate's Fiat outside her Indiana University apartment in Willkie Quad's Mason Hall. Courtesy of the author.

Fig. 10. Barbara and I in the back of a limousine after our wedding at St. Andrew the Apostle Catholic Church. Courtesy of the author.

Fig. 11. With Dad and Mom and holding a Stroh's celebrating my graduation from the McKinney School of Law, just four months before Dad died. Courtesy of the author.

Fig. 12. *Indianapolis Star* picture of playing basketball at the governor's residence with Governor Evan Bayh (*far right,* fouling me), Secretary of State (and future Indianapolis mayor) Joe Hogsett, and gubernatorial staffer (and future Marion County prosecutor and Indiana attorney general) Jeff Modisett (*far left*). Evan's inscription reads: "To my good friend Fred 'Kareem' Glass: Thanks for helping prove that this administration is strong on defense!! Best wishes, Evan Bayh." Credit: USA Today Network.

To Fred with deep appreciation for your friendship and help!
Birch Bayh

Fig. 13. My internship "grip and grin" photo with my political hero Senator Birch Bayh. Courtesy of the author.

Fig. 14. With President Bill Clinton as his Indiana campaign chair. Public domain.

Fig. 15. All the Glasses at President Clinton's second inauguration. From *left to right*: George (with Bear), Joey, me, Connor, Barbara, and Katie. Former Indianapolis mayor Bart Peterson's wife, Amy, can be seen behind Katie. Courtesy of the author.

Fig. 16. A photo from the *Indianapolis Star* of Mayor-elect Peterson at a news conference with me and his newly appointed cabinet. Credit: Matt Kryger, USA Today Network.

*(right)* Fig. 17. Securing an "extraordinary project," even though not exactly the way we had planned. Credit: USA Today Network.

GOOD NEWS FOR GAME 4
Reggie's on a roll for Pacers; Celtics' Walker (right) suspended. D1

 DEAR POPE
Student letters pepper Benedict
with questions, best wishes. B3

# THE INDIANAPOLIS STAR

*"Where the spirit of the Lord is, there is Liberty" 2 Cor. 3:17*

A GANNETT NEWSPAPER ■ INDYSTAR.COM　　■ SATURDAY, APRIL 30, 2005 ■　　CITY FINAL ■ 50 CENTS

# STADIUM WINS, 108-36

■ In the end, easy passage:
House, 62-33; Senate, 46-3

■ 11th-hour vote wraps up
a contentious session

Rendering provided by the city of Indianapolis

■ Plan is to break ground
Aug. 1, open arena in '08

■ Convention Center
will spread onto Dome site

## Huddles, audibles and lots of rushing

The final day of negotiations over a new Colts stadium had all of the drama of a classic football game (times are approximate):

**10:30 a.m.:** Gov. Mitch Daniels says talks are faltering. "Your stadium is about to go down," he tells an Indianapolis reporter.

**11:34 a.m.:** The governor calls Mayor Bart Peterson, urging him to rally Democrats behind the bill.

**1 p.m.:** Sen. Luke Kenley, R-Noblesville, says there appears to be support for the bill in the Senate but cautions that it is being revised with less than 12 hours left in the session.

**1:30 p.m.:** With many Republicans opposed to the bill's tax increases, House Speaker Brian Bosma warns it will fail in the House without as many as 20 Democratic votes.

**3 p.m.:** Indianapolis Deputy Mayor Steve Campbell shoots back at Republicans who say the mayor isn't working hard for the bill. "Three years of work isn't enough?" he said of Peterson's talks with the Colts and GOP lawmakers.

**5 p.m.:** The mayor arrives at the Statehouse for a last-ditch push.

**7 p.m.:** With concessions on two issues from Republicans, the mayor announces a deal has been reached.

**10:40 p.m.:** The House passes the stadium bill 62-33, following the Senate's 46-3 vote.

**Late-night victory:** Indianapolis Mayor Bart Peterson (right) and Deputy Mayor Steve Campbell (left) watched House members pass the Colts stadium bill as the clock neared 11 Friday night. "This is really an extraordinary project," Peterson said.
*Charlie Nye / The Star*

### By Matthew Tully
matthew.tully@indystar.com

After four months of sometimes angry debate, the General Assembly took a crucial step toward solidifying the city's NFL future Friday night by easily approving a financing plan for a new Colts stadium and expanded Indiana Convention Center.

The vote paves the way for the start of one of the biggest public works projects in Indianapolis history and appears to end years of questions about whether the Colts are here to stay.

"We are going to expand the Convention Center, and we are going to build a new stadium for the Indianapolis Colts to play in for 30 more years," Indianapolis Mayor Bart Peterson said. "This is really an extraordinary project."

It was also an extraordinary debate, one that stretched back to 2002, when the mayor began formal negotiations with Colts owner Jim Irsay. At times, many wondered whether the Colts were going to leave for Los Angeles or elsewhere in search of a bigger market and greater riches.

But after years of uncertainty, it appears Colts fans can relax.

"There is still much to be accomplished and many issues to be resolved before the new venue becomes a reality," Irsay said in a statement. "But tonight the project has taken a big step forward."

As the mayor watched from behind a glass door outside the chamber, the

*See Stadium, Page A13*

---

## Time will tell about lawmaker's DST vote

### By Mary Beth Schneider
mary.beth.schneider@indystar.com

After Rep. Troy Woodruff cast the deciding vote Thursday night to put Indiana on daylight-saving time, he had two phone conversations.

He spoke with Gov. Mitch Daniels, who was delighted.

He spoke with his wife, Melissa, who was not.

"She was angry," the Vincennes Republican said with a rueful laugh.

He knew his vote would make her and many of his constituents in his southwestern Indiana district mad. Chances are he won't lose her vote over the issue, but the others are dicey.

Part of the district, including his home, is in the Eastern time zone,

and part of it is in the Central time zone. Many of the folks he represents have to split their lives between the two zones.

Including, at times, his wife. The corporate headquarters of her employer is in St. Louis, in the Central time zone. Without daylight-saving time, her business and home are in sync from April through October. With the time

change, the office and home always will operate an hour apart.

Unless, that is, Woodruff's southwestern district is moved to the Central time zone, too.

"I promised her I'd do whatever I can to make that happen," Woodruff said.

The bill he voted for, and which

*See Time, Page A13*

**Rep. Troy Woodruff** cast the decisive vote Thursday night.

### More legislative news

■ **Indy Works altered:** A modified plan to consolidate local government is approved. B1
■ **Budget approved:** A tight two-year budget gets the green light. B7
■ **Meth bill passes:** Cold medicine will be out of easy reach under legislation that was approved unanimously. B7

### On the Web

Go to IndyStar.com to see what Gov. Mitch Daniels said at a 10:30 a.m. news conference today.

---

## Hoosier cyclist dies 1 day after ride of a lifetime

### By Rob Schneider
rob.schneider@indystar.com

Bicycling was Broc Bebout's ticket to good health after heart bypass surgery, and his cross-country ride was a testament to the power of pedaling.

But on Thursday, the day after he completed the 2,400-mile journey from Carlsbad, Calif., to Brunswick, Ga., Bebout died on the van ride back to his Anderson home.

In an e-mail to his wife a little after 4 p.m. Wednesday, before he

and his companions went out for a celebratory steak dinner, the 57-year-old Bebout wrote about what the trip had meant to him.

"Right now I'm anxious to get home but still sad that it's over," he said of the cross-country trip. "An incredible experience with incredible people."

Patricia Brinkman, Bebout's wife, said her husband seemed to be thriving on the ride when she joined him for a 60-mile leg last Wednesday that his cross-country journey was "incredible."

*See Cyclist, Page A12*

**A passion for pedaling:** Broc Bebout, of Anderson, e-mailed his wife Wednesday that his cross-country journey was "incredible."
*Undated photo provided by Patricia Brinkman*

---

### COMING SUNDAY

**Parents' silence can have tragic cost**

Too often child abuse at the hands of a spouse, boyfriend or girlfriend is ignored, with deadly consequences.

**Small groups hold big churches together**

Worshippers in massive congregations say the real ministry often is found in more personal settings.

---

## A bloody day in Iraq: 17 blasts, 50 people dead

### By Thomas Wagner
Associated Press

BAGHDAD, Iraq — Insurgents set off at least 17 bombs in Iraq on Friday, killing at least 50 people, including three U.S. soldiers, in a series of attacks aimed at shaking Iraq's newly formed government.

An audiotape by one of America's most-wanted insurgents, Abu Musab al-Zarqawi, warned President Bush that more bloodshed was to come.

The well-coordinated attacks, which also wounded 114 Iraqis

and seven Americans, came as political leaders are trying to curb the insurgency by including all of Iraq's main religious and ethnic groups into an uncertain new Shiite-dominated government, which will take office Tuesday.

Most of the bombing targets were Iraqi security forces and police, whom insurgents accuse of collaborating with the Americans.

An association of Sunni Muslim clerics believed to have links

*See Bombs, Page A12*

---

Fig. 18. Outside my office with the sign not only modeling accessibility for the department but facilitating my favorite part of the job: getting to know our students. Photograph by Rodney Margison, courtesy of *Bloom Magazine*.

Fig. 19. Reconciling with the IU 10, one of my most meaningful experiences of my time as IU AD. From *left to right*: Gordon May, Clarence Price, Larry Highbaugh, Mike Adams, me, Charlie Murphy, Benny Norman, and Don Silas. Courtesy of Indiana University Athletics.

Fig. 20. Sewing seeds for his transformative $5 million gift by outfitting Mark Cuban in IU gear at a presentation he made in Bloomington for the Kelley School of Business. Courtesy of Indiana University Athletics.

Fig. 21. With President Obama, President McRobbie, and IU's 2013 national champion men's soccer team at the White House. Public domain.

Fig. 22. Presenting the game ball to Coach Tom Allen after beating Nebraska in 2019. Note Tom's middle linebacker son Thomas in the lower right-hand corner, proudly looking up at his dad. Courtesy of Indiana University Athletics.

Fig. 23. My guy wide receiver Whop Philyor and his guy Chucky before the Walk at a 2019 home game. Courtesy of Indiana University Athletics.

Fig. 24. Referee Ted Valentine confirming Christian Watford's three-pointer to beat number one Kentucky as Coach Crean looks on. I apparently didn't need any confirmation. Courtesy of Indiana University Athletics.

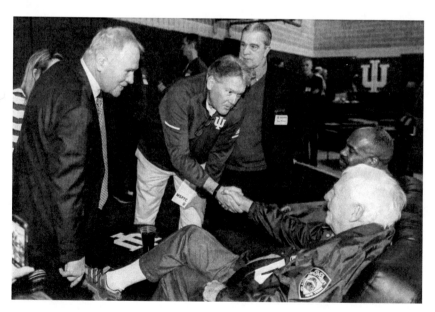

Fig. 25. Welcoming back Coach Knight with doctors Larry Rink and (also former player) Steve Ahlfeld as the legend sits with former player Dean Garrett. Courtesy of Indiana University Athletics.

Fig. 26. Sharing an IU men's basketball game with (*left to right*) Barbara; Katie; George; Joe; his future wife, Emily; Katie's husband, Tom; and Connor, one of my favorite things to do as IU AD. Courtesy of Indiana University Athletics.

Fig. 27. A photo from the *Indianapolis Star* of me with my first grandchild, Betsy, at an IU Athletics event. By the time I left IU, I had gone from no grandchildren to five and was always looking for opportunities to share my role with them. Credit: Matt Detrich, USA Today Network.

# *OPPORTUNITY*

# 8. SERVING A GOVERNOR

Shortly after the 1988 election, I got a telephone call that Governor-elect Evan Bayh wanted to meet with me. I assumed he just wanted to thank me for the work I had done on his campaign. Barbara asked me if I thought he might offer me a job, and I said no. Besides, I was very happy as a young associate practicing law at Callahan & Riley. But when Evan offered me a position in the governor's office on his senior staff, I called Barbara to tell her I was going to take it. She was not surprised. He asked me to be the "executive assistant for transportation" overseeing the Highway Department, Bureau of Motor Vehicles, and the Port Commission. At first I asked him if he was sure, noting I really didn't know anything about those issues and that I was a lawyer, not an engineer. He told me he wasn't hiring me for my knowledge but rather for my judgment, which he had come to trust while I worked on issues during his campaign. Even though I frankly didn't feel prepared or even competent for my job, I had the confidence to take it because Evan, my boss, believed I could do it. Accept opportunities presented to you even if you're not sure you are ready, or even capable, because all that matters is that the person offering you the opportunity obviously believes you are. This was the first of what turned out to be many replays of this kind of analysis for me, including at least twice more in the governor's office when Evan asked me first to become his deputy chief of staff and later chief of staff.

It was heady stuff for a twenty-nine-year-old. But Evan was only thirty-two, and it had been twenty-four years since a Democrat had been elected governor in Indiana, so there were opportunities for young, inexperienced whippersnappers like me. With Evan's election, Indiana would go from having the nation's oldest governor to its youngest, displacing a guy named Bill Clinton. The staff Evan assembled was amazing and included great diversity in experience, gender, race, and life. Among that initial staff were a future Indianapolis mayor; Marion County prosecutor; two Indiana attorneys general; a federal district court judge and court of appeals judge; Indiana Supreme Court justice; Indiana State Democratic Party chair; and a myriad of other future business, legal, and political leaders. Ultimately, I think our relative youth and inexperience served us well, for although they fostered some rookie mistakes, those were more than set off by the ambitious, idealistic agenda we largely successfully pursued, being too naive to know we couldn't or shouldn't.

At that time (unlike now), we had a large and active statehouse press corps aggressively covering the administration, looking for and chronicling our missteps. While that could be challenging, we were sometimes the beneficiaries of the public's interest, and therefore the media's interest, in this new handsome, vigorous governor. For example, early in the administration, Evan put up a basketball hoop in the driveway of the governor's residence, and the *Indianapolis Star* did a big story about it, complete with a picture of the governor playing two-on-two with me, future Indianapolis mayor Joe Hogsett, and future Marion County prosecutor and Indiana attorney general Jeff Modisett. I was quite the loser in this group.

A variety of circumstances came into play to put me in that game and to have gotten that call from Evan. These include, most significantly, my 1980 Senate internship with his father and his father's 1980 reelection campaign and my engagement in Evan's campaigns for secretary of state and governor, which arose from those 1980 experiences.

\* \* \*

Toward the end of my junior year at IU, I had decided I wanted to pursue an internship that summer with Congress. My girlfriend went with me and waited outside as I went to see my academic advisor in the Student Building to tell her of my ambition. Of course, my advisor laughed at me that I was pursuing this so late, as was fairly typical of me at this time in my life. She did tell me about a fall internship with Senator Birch Bayh on the Judiciary Committee's Subcommittee on the Constitution, which he chaired, for which I could apply. She told me that Senator Bayh reserved at least one intern position on the subcommittee for a Hoosier so that they didn't all get taken up by kids from Georgetown and George Washington Universities. I went back outside and told my girlfriend what I had learned. I was initially intrigued, as Senator Bayh was a political hero of mine, but fairly quickly I started to give a million excuses why I couldn't do it. I didn't want to miss the fall of my senior year at IU. I wouldn't be able to graduate on time if I didn't take classes in the fall. I wanted to work for the senator's personal staff, not this chumpy "subcommittee." It felt really good sliding back into my comfort zone. To my surprise and dismay, my girlfriend didn't accept my excuses; she challenged them. "You could take classes in the summer and still graduate on time. The subcommittee sounds interesting. I thought you wanted to be a lawyer. This would be great for that!" I applied and was selected for the internship, and that girl from college is still my girlfriend—we've been married for nearly forty years.

Ever since I had been a little kid, I had envisioned Washington, DC, as this magical place made up of special people using their extraordinary abilities to discern public policy, pass legislation, and lead. The most critical, fundamental, and valuable lesson of my internship was that Washington wasn't about magic at all. It's made up of ordinary people with ordinary abilities who put themselves in the fray, work hard, and are committed to getting things done. The revelation to me was that I could do this.

Virtually all the great professional opportunities I've gotten since can be tied to that internship and the self-confidence I gained from doing it. I wouldn't have had that experience if not for a friend's loving nudge and a US senator who didn't forget where he came from. It was also the first, or at least the most memorable, example of perhaps the most important precept to making your own luck: Opportunities often come at inconvenient times. Don't let that prevent you from seizing them. Find a way. If you don't resist passing on an opportunity because it is not a convenient time to pursue it, you are simply going to miss most of them and, consequently, miss out on those experiences that make life the most fulfilling and fun.

When I reported to the Subcommittee on the Constitution, I found out I had been reassigned to a new ad hoc subcommittee that Senator Bayh was now chairing: the Subcommittee to Investigate Individuals Representing the Interest of Foreign Governments, also known as the Billy Carter Committee. Allegations, which seem quite tame through the current prism of rampant family self-dealing and inappropriate foreign engagement in the Trump White House, had arisen regarding President Carter's ne'er-do-well brother Billy's involvement with the Libyan government. Normally such allegations would have been investigated by the Senate Judiciary Committee, but its chairman, Ted Kennedy, was running against President Carter for the Democratic nomination for president, so he recused himself, leaving it to Senator Bayh to chair the special committee. He agreed to do so at significant personal political cost, as it's rarely popular to be investigating a president of your own party, although the opposite is true. Ask Sam Ervin. Also, it was not helpful for Birch Bayh, a master retail politician, to be stuck in Washington in an election year, especially in a role that portrayed him as part of the Washington establishment at a time when that was particularly unpopular.

I was at first naively disappointed with my reassignment. Ultimately, however, I came to understand that this could be a great opportunity, and I threw myself into my new role. Our greatest disappointments can create our greatest opportunities if we don't let them deter us. It was very high profile with constant and direct involvement of not only Senator Bayh but a who's who of members of the Senate, including Senators Richard Lugar, Bob Dole, Pat Leahy, Claiborne Pell, and Strom Thurmond, among others. It was on a fast track to be completed in advance of the election, so there was lots going on and lots to do, especially compared with the normally quiet summer congressional calendar. There were many hearings. Occasionally, I had the opportunity to staff Senator Bayh to and from the hearing room, making sure he got everywhere on time and handling any issues that might come up. The first time, he had to stop in the bathroom, and I demurred, telling him I didn't have to go. He told me, "Son, I'm going to give you your first political lesson: Never skip an opportunity to use the bathroom because you never know when the next opportunity will be coming along." I have followed that great advice the rest of my life, in politics and out. I often ran the "Pell Lights." The brainchild of Senator Claiborne Pell of Rhode Island, it was a set of green, yellow, and red lights that tracked a senator's time for questioning witnesses. Many was the time the light would go red, and Chairman Bayh would give me a little wink to turn it off so as not to embarrass a colleague.

I occasionally was asked to hand-deliver documents to the subcommittee members personally to try to ensure confidentiality, which was not a hallmark of this committee. Once when I delivered some documents to Senator Pat Leahy of Vermont, he yelled at me, rhetorically, I think, "Who the hell is leaking this stuff?"

A major issue was whether the president would have to testify before the subcommittee. Sound familiar? Eventually a compromise was reached where President Carter agreed to answer written questions. Shortly thereafter, I was told to deliver a package to White House Counsel Lloyd Cutler at the Old Executive Office Building and "insist on putting it directly in his hands." I was driven there by two Capitol Hill police officers in their cruiser. They were listening to the news on the car radio, and the newscaster said: "As we speak, the congressional interrogatories are being delivered to the White House." That's when I realized that I had them, that *I* was delivering this rather historic document. When I got to the OEOB, I asked for Mr. Cutler, and I remember him walking toward me at the reception desk down a long corridor that seemed to take him forever. He was dashing, professional, and curt, and—while some may have considered this to be a mundane errand—as I was riding back with my police escorts, I realized I was catching the fever of being where the action is.

Along those same lines, the night before the subcommittee's report was to be released, I was assigned to being personally stationed in the Senate printing room all night to make sure no copies were prematurely released and no one came in to read the report before it was released the next morning. Thousands of copies of the report would be printed, and I was told to be prepared to stay there, awake, all night. I was, and I did. It turns out there was a disagreement among the senators on the subcommittee as to what specific words to use to characterize/criticize the conduct of Billy Carter and the administration. There were actually two alternatives printed for the same page of the report with only those very few words being different. In the wee hours of the morning, I got the call from my boss with the subcommittee staff telling me which page to plug in. I confess to feeling pretty important when I shared that with the printing staff, who by that time had become my guys.

The subcommittee's report was released that next day on October 2, 1980, and Senator Bayh rushed back to Indiana to campaign before the quickly approaching election. I also went back to Indiana to work on the campaign with Barbara. Of course, it was all for naught, as Senator Bayh was swept aside in the Reagan landslide by a young, obscure, but well-connected congressman, Dan Quayle. A number of other lions of the Senate went down in defeat that year: Frank Church of Idaho, George McGovern of South Dakota, and Warren Magnuson of Washington, among others. Later, a fellow intern who was working on the Judiciary Committee for Senator Kennedy told me that he was watching the returns with his office colleagues, who were sympathetically, but somewhat clinically, sad when they saw Senator Bayh lost but then devastated when it hit home that the Democrats were losing control of the Senate and they would all be out of jobs!

Right after the election, I was in an all-staff meeting with Senator Bayh in which he was remarkably upbeat, encouraging, and optimistic and, among other things, called on his now lame-duck, soon-to-be-unemployed staff to do everything they could to get passed what would become the landmark bipartisan Bayh-Dole Act, with Republican Senator Bob Dole of Kansas. I'm embarrassed to say it wasn't until I returned to

Indiana University as a vice president that I realized how critical that legislation has been to driving innovation and economic development through enhanced application of inventions developed from federal government–funded research, especially at universities. Senator Bayh could have quietly licked his wounds and stayed out of the fray, scorned by the electorate. Instead, he went back to work and used his time to keep getting important things done.

After my internship and the 1980 election, I returned to Bloomington for my final semester, which included completing my paper based on the internship to secure the nine hours credit I would receive for it and that I needed to graduate. It was titled "Birch Bayh: An Exception to the Electoral Connection" and essentially argued that, unlike most politicians, Birch Bayh prioritized doing the right thing above reelection. This explained why a senator from a conservative state would successfully spearhead the fight against not one but two conservative, unqualified Supreme Court nominees; support federally funded abortions and thus a woman's right to choose, rich or poor; successfully sponsor constitutional amendments to give eighteen-year-olds the right to vote and clarify presidential succession; unsuccessfully sponsor the Equal Rights Amendment (although it was passed by Congress); and chair the Billy Carter Committee. In the paper, I concluded that "I hope for the sake of Congress and the nation that more exceptions like Birch Bayh emerge and manage to survive." I'll keep hoping.

* * *

My internship experience helped me to get connected with Evan Bayh and his closest associates as he was preparing for his first campaign, for Indiana Secretary of State in 1986. Evan had campaigned for Wayne Townsend in his 1984 gubernatorial race, and Bill Moreau had been the campaign's counsel. I had gotten to know Bill in 1980 through the Birch Bayh internship. Joe Hogsett, a close confidant of Bill's and associate of Evan's, was chair of the Marion County Voter Protection Program and had worked tirelessly in 1984 to counteract aggressive and well-organized voter suppression efforts by Marion County Republicans. I worked in that and many future Voter Protection Program efforts.

This is where I first got to know Joe, who has become one of my closest friends and political confidants. Joe was later elected mayor of Indianapolis in 2015 and reelected four years later. He has been an outstanding mayor. The city is fortunate that he has been willing to serve at great personal financial sacrifice. In these polarizing political times, he has reached across the aisle to secure bipartisan support for initiatives such as the new community justice center, a new headquarters hotel, the expansion of the convention center, and balanced city budgets, all in the midst of the unprecedented challenges of the COVID-19 pandemic and social unrest arising from George Floyd's murder.

Sue Cook had been Birch Bayh's volunteer coordinator in 1980 and was an important member of the extended Bayh family, including being a leading ERA advocate in Indiana. In 1985, Sue hosted a small event billed as a post-wedding party for Evan and Susan, but I've always suspected it was to bring together a group of people who might get involved in the 1986 secretary of state campaign. It certainly was the main topic of conversation.

Arising out of relationships reestablished at that party, Barbara was the first to get involved politically with Evan. She volunteered on both his campaigns for secretary of state and governor. In the governor's race, she served as Susan's scheduler. I still remember the box of graham crackers Barbara kept by the phone for our two-year-old, Joey, to keep him from crying when she was on the phone at home scheduling Susan. When the phone rang, he would start kicking his arms and legs and licking his lips, a little like Pavlov's dog. Barbara later served on Evan Bayh's senior secretary of state staff. For those who assume that I helped Barbara get involved in public service, I'm quick to point out that the opposite is true. She was there first!

Barbara and I and our friends Mary Solada and Marci Reddick cohosted the very first fundraiser for Evan's secretary of state campaign on September 26, 1985, at Mary's house. The requested donation was the princely sum of twenty-five dollars per person. We were amazed and thrilled when my Brebeuf buddy John Dillon (whose dad had been Indiana attorney general and for whom Dad had worked as an investigator) gave us a $100 contribution, which put us over our $1,000 goal for the event. That both the hosts and the candidate were so pleased with such a comparatively small amount of money is a testament to how far political fundraising has come and how early it was in this campaign.

Bit by bit on the secretary of state campaign, primarily through Barbara, I started to be assigned a variety of seemingly mundane tasks, the most exciting of which was staffing the candidate himself. I was driving him to a number of events throughout Southern Indiana when Barbara was close to being due with our first child, Katie. My kids were prenatal Democrats too! In that pre–cell phone era, at every stop I would find a phone and call Barbara to see how she was doing. Evan would tell the audience what I was doing, as people love baby stories, and then he started weaving it into his remarks: "I'm running so that Fred's new baby will be able to have a bright future in the state of Indiana." She has, by the way.

Successfully cohosting the first fundraiser for Evan Bayh's secretary of state's race, even with a fairly modest $1,000 take, and getting to know Evan personally by volunteering to drive him around whenever I could were important elements of developing my political role with him and his staff. Another seemingly pedestrian but important milestone came early in his campaign for governor. That campaign was run by the triumvirate of Evan Bayh, Bill Moreau, and Joe Hogsett. There was also an "advisory committee" of volunteers who got together on a regular basis, which included me and John Dillon, among many others. The committee was full of good and capable people, but it was definitely several steps removed from the real action of the campaign.

At one of the committee's early meetings, Joe said he wanted Evan to have a presence at the 1987 state Democratic Jefferson-Jackson Day Dinner, which was particularly important since at that time Evan was still in a contested primary for the nomination for governor. John and I saw this as our chance. We offered to run it, and Joe agreed. I've always thought he was unsure if these two young bucks could pull it off. We made it our mission and sole focus to show that we could. We formed our own "Evan Bayh Jefferson-Jackson Dinner Committee" and installed ourselves as cochairs. We organized a Bayh event outside the dinner that we billed as a wedding reception for Evan and Susan to "celebrate a new beginning for them and Indiana," complete with a cake! We had multiple, detailed meetings, with written minutes setting up staffing assignments, displays, thank-you cards, "mingling" instructions, campaign button distribution, and the like. In short, we killed it. We overkilled it. We were getting the candidate's attention and that of the rest of the triumvirate. After that, John, Barbara, and I became a more go-to part of the campaign. Pursuing every opportunity I could get on Evan's secretary of state and gubernatorial campaigns and attacking them with creativity and energy resulted in that call for the meeting with Evan and the breakthrough of my career. Seize every opportunity to the fullest. Own it. Exceed expectations. Confirm the confidence that has been placed in you and show that you are capable of even more.

Additional benefits of working on Evan's campaigns were the opportunities to interact with Birch, who was always available to consult on the campaign as well as help campaign himself. I once told him how much I appreciated the opportunity to work for Evan. He told me in return that a lot of great people had done a lot of great things for him during his career and that he sincerely appreciated them all, but you never appreciate what people do for you as much as you appreciate what they do for your children, and then he thanked me! His observation is so true, and I have kept it in mind, as over the years I have tried to go out of my way to help the children of my friends and associates and to be sure to express my appreciation when they have helped mine.

Evan prevailed on election day, becoming the first Democrat elected governor of Indiana in twenty-four years. Barbara and I were thrilled and stayed up all night celebrating at the downtown headquarters hotel for the Bayh campaign. When we got home around seven o'clock the next morning, without having slept, I begged Mom to skip work to keep watching our two little ones for us, offering her a million dollars she knew I didn't have if she would. She demurred, and Barbara and I had a rough day, but it was certainly worth it.

* * *

Although I had been interested in politics my entire life and was just coming off being fairly involved in a statewide gubernatorial campaign, I was about to enter an invaluable, intense master course in real politics.

Party Democrats from around the state expected the change in the party controlling the governor's office to have the same government employment ramifications as the last time it had switched twenty years prior in 1968. Lore had it that the incoming Republican administration went through the Indiana State Office Building floor by floor firing incumbent Democratic workers to be replaced with loyal Republicans. Democratic county chairmen were walking into their local license branches, measuring the windows for new drapes and purporting to fire the Republican workers. But it was a new day. Not only had federal case law changed to limit the ability for government employers to consider politics for almost all rank-and-file jobs, but Evan had run on—and was serious about—cleaning up what he saw as partisan political hiring abuses of the previous administration. As the executive assistant for transportation, overseeing two of the historically most politically partisan agencies in state government in the Department of Highways and the Bureau of Motor Vehicles, I stood as a neophyte at ground zero of the clash of expectations and reality for party Democrats all over the state of Indiana.

Even before Evan's term officially began, we were inundated with people interested in positions in the new administration, including a lot of guys like the one who told Evan during the campaign, "I'm tired of working for a living. I want me one of them state jobs." There was particular interest in jobs as license branch managers and subdistrict highway superintendents, for which we were confident politics could and should be a consideration given that they were policymaking in nature. In fact, we felt it was our responsibility to get people in those jobs who were committed to carrying out the policies of the new administration. That is why we were so aggressive in trying to replace the leadership of the agencies that we believed had been more beholden to its political party than the overall people of Indiana.

This started at the top when Evan Bayh plucked Chris Letts, a dynamo of a woman, from the senior executive ranks of Cummins Engine to be his first commissioner of the Department of Highways, replacing the previous commissioner who had simultaneously been serving as a Republican Party district chairman. Chris's appointment was a shock to many, as she was not an engineer, a politician, or a man. She was a nonpolitical, Harvard-educated female superstar. Evan broke this glass ceiling to appoint a proven leader and expert at organizational management to deliver more efficient services to the public. I was told that women in the Highway Department actually danced on their chairs when they heard the news of Chris's appointment. With Chris's help, we set about trying to bring additional professional new blood into the department's leadership, particularly the district engineers and subdistrict superintendents, which we renamed managers to reflect our desire to attract professional managers to those posts.

I was sued along with some other administration officials in federal court by John Selch, who had been the Greenfield subdistrict highway superintendent until he was fired in June 1989. Mr. Selch alleged that politics had been impermissibly considered in his firing. Our position was that although he was not fired for political reasons (rather it was because of his bad attitude and performance), he *could* be fired for political reasons, as those positions were policymaking critical to enacting the policies of the new administration. I always thought that Selch, who had previously pleaded guilty to conspiracy to commit mail fraud in federal court and served time in prison, had a lot of nerve bringing this lawsuit claiming that politics shouldn't be considered with regard to these positions. He had submitted a political clearance card to get his job with the Department of Highways in the first place, and he interviewed for a lower-level job after Evan was elected in apparent recognition that his higher-level job would then be subject to change.

In any event, the matter went to trial, and I testified. I was frustrated by a great deal of the plaintiff's case, which emphasized that he was the choice of professional highway contractors and vendors and that I should have reached out to them to get—and accept—their recommendation of him. From my perspective, we had just won an election rejecting the status quo and authorizing, if not mandating, a new way of looking at things, such as hiring a professional manager as opposed to someone beholden to those he is responsible for managing. This had been the thinking when Evan broke the mold for his new Highway Department commissioner by hiring Chris. Ultimately, Judge Tinder ruled that we had used political considerations in selecting the Greenfield subdistrict superintendent but that the law allowed us to do so because of the policymaking nature of the position. Exoneration! Sort of.

It could be tough in this political environment, where we couldn't meet the pent-up political frustrations of our party members who had been out so long. It was hard to blame them given how the last change of governor's party could be and was handled. In coffee shops and barbershops across the state, incumbent, burrowed-in Republicans were laughing at local Democrats' inability to take their jobs. Early in the Bayh administration, my governor's office colleagues and I went to a meeting of Democratic Party leaders in Southern Indiana. We were getting ripped up one side and down the other. I brazenly, but surprisingly successfully, tried to ingratiate myself with them by pronouncing, "You know I married a little gal from just down [US] Fifty there in Loogootee."

Now, while Barbara's dad grew up in Loogootee, he hadn't lived there in about forty years, and needless to say Barbara never did. My friends appreciated the life preserver, but Barbara was none too happy, especially when she would run into real Loogootee people who would ask, "Now, honey, whereabouts do you live in Loogootee?"

My friend and colleague Bart Peterson was the governor's executive assistant for the environment, which included overseeing the Indiana Department of Environmental Management and the Indiana Department of Natural Resources. Being more of a policy wonk, Bart was sometimes surprised by some of the real-life fallout of the operation of his agencies. For example, once a Southern Indiana mayor called Bart to complain about IDEM enforcing long-ignored clean water regulations in his community with the opener, "Peterson, I'm down here getting my ass eat!" That's not a typo.

The DNR was as political an agency as the ones I oversaw given that the state parks had all been staffed as political jobs. Bart was quizzical as to why there was such high interest in these fairly low-paid positions. He said there was all-out war over a summer concession contract that wasn't worth anything. "You don't understand, Bart," I said. "It's not about the money.

It's about who gets to decide who gets a second squirt of syrup in their snow cones at the snack bar. It had been the Republicans. The Democrats want it to be them!" I do think that's it in a nutshell.

* * *

In the movie *Thirteen Days*, about the Cuban Missile Crisis, the young and comparatively inexperienced Kennedy team decides to seek the advice of former Secretary of State Dean Acheson about how to react to the Soviet Union placing nuclear missiles in Cuba. Acheson's bellicose counsel is for airstrikes and an invasion of Cuba, which Kennedy knows could well lead to nuclear war with the Soviet Union. After meeting with Acheson, President Kennedy is dismayed by his advice, but notes Acheson has more experience with the Soviets than anyone. Kennedy's friend and senior staffer Kenny O'Donnell tells the president, "There is no expert on the subject. There is no wise old man. There's just us."

After recalling his regret deferring to military and diplomatic "experts" in authorizing the disastrous Cuban Bay of Pigs Invasion, President Kennedy then says, "There's something immoral about abandoning your own judgment."

Similarly, I quickly learned in the governor's office that we couldn't and shouldn't delegate our responsibility to make decisions even if we felt inadequate to make them. Evan expected us to get as much information and counsel as possible, but ultimately to trust our own instincts, including when, as was usual, we had to make decisions sooner than we would like based on less information than we wanted. The people of the state of Indiana had given Evan, and by extension us staffers, that responsibility. Over time, I became confident in making those decisions and not looking for a wise old man to do it for me. Accept opportunities presented to you even if you're not sure you are ready, or even capable, because all that matters is that the person offering you the opportunity believes you are.

I also learned working for Evan how to give the governor my best, most candid counsel and then leave it up to him whether to take it. It's critical not to have too much ownership in your advice. Maybe the Jesuits would call it detachment. I'd done my part in giving my best advice, and I was at peace whether my counsel was followed or not. I've replicated this successful approach with other principals, including officeholders, candidates, clients, and even family members. I often find that the more I reflect my nondefensive acceptance of my advice potentially not being taken, the more seriously that advice is considered. I have kept the pledge of my eight-year-old self to tell my bosses the truth.

In 1991, during tough economic times for the state, Evan's proposed two-year budget bill included no pay raises for state employees, and, boy, were they unhappy. I drafted a "Dear Fellow State Employee" letter from Evan to send to every state employee explaining why, because of the state's financial condition, they wouldn't be getting a raise, but—good news— they would be able to keep their jobs! It didn't go over very well. The State House was littered with crumpled-up copies of the letter. Yes, letters— no email yet. We were inundated with snarky response letters. One guy sent back his letter with a message for the governor scrawled across the top: "You must have balls the size of basketballs if you think we are dumb enough to actually believe this crap."

Our mailroom folks gave it to me, and I forwarded it to the governor with a Post-it Note on which I had written, "We've gotten a lot of negative responses to your letter, but I thought you might want to see a complimentary one."

It was also in the context of the 1991 financial crisis that Evan first told me, "If you have to stick your hand in a meat grinder, just do it once and make sure that it's worth it." In other words, if you are going to incur some political or other pain, take it all at the same time and make sure you get at least as much benefit from doing so. This saying often goes hand in hand with its sister saying, "In for a dime, in for a dollar"; that is, if you're going to take the heat for a little bit, there's often not that much more incremental heat to do a lot, which normally also creates a lot more benefit. In the context of the financial crisis, for example, if you were going to cut an agency's budget by 10 percent and take all the criticism from employees, special interests, legislators, lobbyists, newspapers, political opponents, and the like, you might as well cut it 20 percent. There's twice as much benefit, and the grief you take is about the same.

A variety of tricky matters confronting the administration would make their way to my desk. For example, when Evan was running for reelection in 1992, his opponent, the sitting Indiana attorney general, embraced a platform being used by Republicans around the country attacking tax-payer money being spent on the arts, especially what they deemed to be offensive art funded by the National Endowment for the Arts and similar entities. Indiana state government had its own art commission, most of the members of which were appointed by the governor. Understandably, the commission didn't like the case Evan's opponent was making against public funding of the arts. While Evan was sympathetic to the commission's position, he didn't want to gratuitously feed into his opponent's criticism, so he dispatched me to tell them not to stir the pot on this. These were passionate true believers in uncensored, publicly funded arts and were clearly not happy being asked to stand down. I didn't realize how unhappy they were until, without notice, they published on the glossy cover of their taxpayer-funded monthly magazine a picture of a sculpture that looked to be a giant marble penis on a pedestal (thereafter referred to by most Bayh staffers as *The Schlong on the Schlab*). When I called Evan to tell him about this development, there was a long pause on the other end before he asked, "Does it have balls?" I advised him that it didn't, and he said, "Well, that's good, isn't it?" His analytical skills were always inspiring.

* * *

One of Evan's many strengths is that he is a great communicator. He would often say to me, "People don't know if you don't tell them." When I later became IU AD, my staff would get sick of me repeating that to them. It has both an internal and external application. Leaders can fall into a trap of somehow thinking that their rank-and-file team members, customers, and the public will somehow know and understand by osmosis the decisions and policies that they and their senior team members have been discussing ad nauseum in the boardroom. They don't do it on purpose. It's just human nature to feel that the thing you have been talking about so much is somehow also known by others and that also somehow they have had the benefit of the evolution of your thinking on the subject. Leaders must be disciplined to remember that this is obviously not the case. Talk to your people. Bring them along. Show the math. Rinse and repeat. You can't just tell them once and check the "communicate" box. You've got to keep hammering home your message. Communicate, communicate, communicate. This is at least as true and important for external audiences. The same rules apply. You can't just announce something, congratulate yourself on a great press release or press conference, and believe everyone has heard and understood your message. The message must be simple and consistent. Evan used to say that by the time we were ready to throw up from having seen the same political commercial over and over, its message was just starting to get through to the public at large.

My colleagues in the governor's office were like family, and our "dad" was Press Secretary Fred Nation, who had served in a similar capacity for Evan's father. Fred was older than most of us and provided us with "adult supervision." He also gave me the best parental advice I've ever gotten. Fred told me that when your kids are hardest to love, that's when they need love the most. How simple, yet true and a great reminder on so many levels! He also told me that even when it seems clear that your kids aren't listening to you, they are. Fred said that when some of his kids were in their twenties, they would play back to him almost verbatim things he said to them that he would have bet anything they had ignored. He counseled me to look past the eye rolls, mumbles, snide remarks, and blank faces to keep communicating with them. Perhaps to my own children's frustration, this was a great reminder and even empowerment to me to keep talking to them.

It was in the governor's office that I resolved to leave work every day at five thirty so I could be home for dinner with my kids. Of course, there were exceptions, but I was pretty good at making sure they were fairly few and far between. This resolution arose from how much I disliked the unpredictability of my own childhood. As a kid, we had no set dinnertime because most nights Mom had no idea when Dad would be home. Often she would cook dinner for the time Dad had promised to be home and then try to keep it warm while she called around the bars looking for him and I paced around reciting my "safe, soon, sober" prayer.

I pledged to myself that when I was a parent, I would try to give my kids stability and predictability that would cultivate their security and confidence. To maintain a reasonable work-life balance, you have to set and honor specific times—with reasonable exceptions—that are dedicated just to your family. In the governor's office, I could easily have worked until eleven o'clock every night—as some of my colleagues did—and still not gotten everything done. My view was this: I'm going to go home at five thirty, even if that was frowned upon by some in the office, to have dinner with my kids and be with them until they go to bed because I wasn't going to get everything done I needed to do by staying late anyway.

Thus, with very few exceptions, throughout my career I came home at the same time every night. Some of my fondest memories are all of us sitting around that table off the kitchen, everyone in their usual place. I loved giving them that stability even though I knew, or thought, that it was something they would simply take for granted. I *wanted* them to take it for granted. Just the way things were. Didn't know any different. Perhaps like them participating in sports at Brebeuf. Which of course was the point just to have that be a part of their lives with all the benefits it provides. A completely unexpected and highly treasured recognition of that practice came during a Christmas dinner conversation at daughter Katie's in-law's home in Atlanta not long after she had married Tom. Maybe it arose out of Tom and her settling into their new two-career marriage. In any event, rather offhandedly, she said, "I didn't think about it at the time, but it's pretty amazing that Dad had these really demanding jobs, but we always had dinner all together the same time every night." Maybe it wasn't taken for granted after all. Always do the right thing, even when no one knows or appreciates that you are and even when the right thing looks to some like the wrong thing.

I am forever indebted to Evan Bayh for all that he taught me about leadership. At a very young age, he provided me a great opportunity to learn, develop, and be involved in things that I felt mattered. He threw me into the deep end to figure things out and make them happen (or not happen!). He would identify his ultimate objective and give me room to figure out how to get there with his involvement usually limited to asking piercing questions that went to the heart of the weakest part of my analysis. In retrospect, I think he gave me that room in part because he really didn't know how to get there either! He was only thirty-two when he was elected governor. He had and has an amazing combination of extraordinary vision, instincts, historical perspective, smarts, and an ambitious desire to do good and important things. I learned a great deal from him, much of which is reflected throughout this book, which I apply often to this very day.

* * *

I had an interesting potential opportunity in 1992, late in my time in the governor's office. Of course, in addition to Evan running for reelection that year, Bill Clinton was successfully challenging incumbent George Bush for the presidency. During that campaign, my then four-year-old Joey asked me, "We want George Bush to die, right, Dad?" Yikes! Memo to self: tone down the political rhetoric at home. In any event, shortly after the election, I got a call from my old boss, Judge Dillin, telling me that he was giving me advance notice that he was planning to retire from active judge status and "to treat that information as you see fit." I knew exactly what he was doing. With a new Democratic president and no Indiana Democratic senators, per tradition, it would fall to Indiana Democratic Governor Evan Bayh to recommend Judge Dillin's life-tenured replacement. Judge Dillin had just given me a head start to put myself in a position to succeed him. For me, it was a dream come true. I always had great admiration for federal district court judges in general and Judge Dillin in particular. I talked to Evan about it, and he told me that if I wanted it, he would support me, which in the end is really all I should need.

Then Bill Clinton nominated Zoe Baird to be the US attorney general. She ended up removing herself from consideration because she had paid her housekeeper in cash and had not withheld any federal or other taxes. Scandals could be so quaint back then. Barbara and I had done the same thing with our babysitter, so, based on the Baird experience, I felt as though I shouldn't pursue the appointment, as it could have embarrassed both Evan and the president and likely been unsuccessful. I note it might have been unsuccessful anyway. I was only thirty-three years old and had actively practiced law less than three years. My colleague David Hamilton, the governor's counsel, was Evan's ultimate nominee. His nomination languished forever for political issues dressed up as questions about his qualifications. He was very clearly qualified and much more qualified than I was. David was ultimately confirmed and has served brilliantly on the federal bench, both at the federal district court and now appellate level.

Not being able to purse that federal district court appointment was a blow and my greatest professional disappointment ever, at least until Bart Peterson lost his third term as mayor of Indianapolis. But, ironically, like Bart's defeat, I believe it turned out to be one of the best things that ever happened to me. In retrospect, I think I would have found that role to be isolating, especially because I'm not really a lawyer who loves the law. I've come to understand what I love is leadership and being in the fray. Had I become a federal district court judge out of the governor's office, I simply wouldn't have had the many career and service opportunities that I have been blessed with since that time. Our greatest disappointments can create our greatest opportunities if we don't let them deter us.

* * *

Evan was elected to a second term with a record 62 percent of the vote, a staggering plurality for a statewide Democrat in Indiana. Working in the governor's office, especially as chief of staff during a reelection campaign, is a demanding, draining job. I had wanted to leave right after the 1992 election, but Evan asked me to stay through the 1993 legislative session, which normally would end in April, and of course I agreed to do so. When you go out, go out the right way. On March 30, 1993, Evan announced my planned departure, saying, "Fred Glass has been a key member of my staff since the beginning of my administration, and as chief of staff supervised the complex and difficult task of tightening the state's administrative belt through the worst of the national recession. I have prevailed on Fred to stay in state service through the present, crucial legislative session." Unluckily for me, it ended up being one of the longest, most acrimonious legislative sessions in history, primarily over the issue of the riverboat gambling legislation, which was ultimately passed over the governor's veto, including multiple special sessions that adjourned months later than normal.

My "ticket out" was my friend and colleague Bart Peterson, whom I had earlier made my deputy chief of staff and later proposed to the governor that he succeed me as chief of staff. You couldn't leave until you identified an acceptable replacement. I had been that for my predecessor, Bill Moreau, and Bart would be that for me. We had the most complete, engaged transition in the history of transitions. For weeks, Bart shadowed me everywhere. We worked on every problem together, shoulder to shoulder.

My last month in the governor's office, I formally changed my role to "special counsel to the governor" as Bart took over as chief of staff so that I could be onsite to support him. As part of that, I even moved out of the chief of staff's office, directly connected to the governor's office, so that Bart could move in and get closer, literally and figuratively, to the governor. He was prepared as prepared could be. Still, a couple of weeks after I formally left the governor's office on July 9, 1993, Bart called me and said, "Why the hell didn't you tell me what this crazy job was like?"

It's so true that with jobs of leadership, you just can't know what it's like until you actually do it. As close as I was to Evan, I'm confident I have no real idea what it was like for him to be governor. Same for Bart when he was mayor. I don't think even those closest to me at IU had any real idea what it felt like to be the athletic director. They say the longest eighteen inches in college basketball is the distance between where the head coach and the assistant coach sit. I think this phenomenon is important for both leaders and those who advise them to keep in mind.

A couple of months after I had left the governor's office, the State House reporter for the *Gary Post Tribune* asked me if I had had a facelift. I guess that job had run me down even more than I realized. Still, I joined the administration at twenty-nine as green as the grass wondering if I would be competent to do the job and left at the ripe old age of thirty-four confident in what I had learned and eager to continue to be involved in public service.

# 9. PRACTICING LAW

When I left the governor's office, I interviewed with five law firms and was fortunate to get five offers. I ended up choosing Baker & Daniels, one of the state's most prestigious law firms, even though, of course, its offer was the lowest of the five. I believed over time it would provide the best opportunity for me, and it undoubtably did. Choose what you judge to be better opportunities over higher salaries. I started work there on July 12, 1993, three days after leaving the governor's office. Ironically, I almost left before I even got started.

I came to Baker & Daniels as a contract partner, meaning that I was simply an employee for two years with the expectation, but not the promise, that at the end of those two years, upon a favorable recommendation of the management committee, I would become a full-fledged equity partner with ownership interest and ownership rights. When I left the governor's office, Evan appointed Barbara to a prominent position in his administration as the vice chair of the Indiana Alcoholic Beverage Commission. I was thrilled! With me finally out of the way, she could accept a position worthy of her abilities.

A few days after my first day, however, I was advised by the management committee that an equity partner, who was also a member of the management committee, had complained that Barbara's status as a member of the Indiana Alcoholic Beverage Commission would impair that partner's practice before the ABC and that they had unanimously voted to tell me to tell Barbara that she needed to resign her position. Can you believe that? Again, the management committee was with whom I had contracted. It set my compensation. It would decide whether I would become an equity partner. It held my professional future in its collective hands. But I never thought twice about telling them that I would just leave and go elsewhere before I would ask her to resign from the ABC. Barbara had sacrificed professional opportunities in government because I was Evan's chief of staff. One of the benefits of me leaving the administration had been that Barbara could then serve in a significant, desirable role such as vice chair of the ABC. I told the management committee that it wasn't 1957 and I didn't need to—and wouldn't—tell my wife what to do with her professional life. Amazingly to me, they were surprised, particularly that I wouldn't even ask her, but after a bit of gnashing of teeth, the management committee reconsidered, and the issue generally faded away. Always do the right thing, even when no one knows or appreciates that you are and even when the right thing looks to some like the wrong thing.

Barbara went on to serve three terms, twelve years, on the ABC under two governors. Over the years, we have continued to be active together formally and informally in politics and public service. Barbara has worked particularly closely with our friend Joe Hogsett, first on Evan's secretary of state and gubernatorial campaigns and later in the secretary of state's office when he was Evan's chief of staff. When Joe was elected mayor in 2015, knowing Barbara to be an exceptional, trustworthy leader, he appointed her to the prestigious Indianapolis Airport Board and supported her election as president. As of this writing, she is still so serving after five years.

In any event, knowing that I was perceived by some at Baker & Daniels as having gotten there more because of my political connections than legal abilities and being off to less than a great start with firm leadership, I knew I had some work to do. Baker & Daniels was one of the most prominent firms in the state, and in 1993, lateral partners were still rather unusual and somewhat frowned upon by the mostly homegrown variety. I had to show I could do Baker & Daniels quality work, and billable hours were the coin of the realm. In my first full year there, I billed more hours than anyone else in a firm full of ambitious, high-performing lawyers. Still, I felt I was at a crossroads. I saw it as a choice between what I preferred to become, a generalist trusted advisor with his own clients who was also active in the community, and becoming a lawyer with a narrow technical legal expertise who would be sought out by others in the firm to serve their clients.

I described this angst to my patient friend Bart Peterson during the drive on our annual pilgrimage to Lambeau Field to see our beloved Green Bay Packers. From our time in the governor's office to this very day, Bart has been one of my most trusted confidants and counsel on professional, and many other, matters. I had concluded that the most prudent course was to find a technical legal niche at which I could become proficient so that I had an expertise they couldn't take away from me. Bart disagreed. He said that although such lawyers were well respected and well paid, they were ultimately commodities producing legal work that could be acquired anywhere. He told me that my judgment and strategic thinking were my strongest attributes and that I should seek out the role of trusted advisor to clients to help them identify and seize opportunities and identify and solve challenges. He predicted doing so would mean getting off the beaten track at a big law firm, but he encouraged me to do so. He conceded that was the riskier and scarier track, but he thought it would lead to a more fun and more lucrative career. Bart knew what he was talking about with regard to big firms, having worked many years at Ice Miller.

I've never forgotten that ride with Bart to Green Bay, and I applied his advice at Baker & Daniels. Despite warnings from many lawyers in the firm, including senior lawyers, but mostly all "commodity lawyers," as Bart had described them, I started focusing more of my time on nonbillable hours in client development and community involvement, political and otherwise, at the expense of the billable hours through which I might have developed a more specific technical expertise.

Although I was focused on pursuing clients, I didn't take every one I could get. After the riverboat legislation passed over Evan's veto, a lot of would-be riverboat license applicants approached me to represent them. It was quite tempting. As a new partner, I understood that these would have been big hits, keeping lots of lawyers busy and generating substantial fees. Ultimately, I decided since I had just left the administration that would ultimately be allocating these licenses, that my representation of these clients could be controversial and potentially embarrassing to Evan. In an August 20, 1993, *Indianapolis Star* article identifying a number of "well-connected Democrats" who were planning to represent entities pursuing riverboat gambling licenses, it noted I had ruled out doing so, quoting me as saying, "Because I have been so recently associated with the governor's office and the administration . . . I just thought that I should sit this one out." In response to that article, I got a call from a sometimes political adversary, Republican State Senator Tom Wyss from Fort Wayne, commending me on passing on that lucrative work when I didn't need to and most wouldn't have. That led to a warm relationship that Tom and I enjoyed for years after. Ironically, by not immediately joining the riverboat license fray, which would have been all-consuming, I gave myself the time to start building a broader practice. Thus, while I passed on the riverboat license work because it was the right thing, it also turned out, as doing the right thing often does, to be the smart thing, as it solidified my reputation for being a person of integrity and ended up helping me build a broader practice. Always do the right thing, even when no one knows or appreciates that you are and even when the right thing looks to some like the wrong thing.

Fortunately, there were lots of clients I did take. Making my own luck, I got clients riding the bus to work and gambling in a casino in Las Vegas, somewhat to the chagrin, but grudging admiration, of my white-shoe colleagues. I represented Martin County, coincidentally the home county of Loogootee, through the county clerk where a private prison was proposing to locate. While predictably controversial, it would have been positive for the county by providing jobs, adding to the tax base, providing the county with its only twenty-four-hour pharmacy, and the like, and my client was for it. There was one particularly active opponent, and I asked my client if she knew any way we could get to him. She said, "Well, we ride the same mule." I thought this was one of those political sayings like "that dog won't hunt," so I asked her to explain. Well, it wasn't a saying. They owned a mule together and took turns riding it!

This matter came to a head when we had a required public hearing in the gymnasium of Shoals High School, which was standing room only with thousands of attendees. I was the facilitator for the county, and we started by having a very professional and compelling presentation by the private prison company. When they were done, we took comments from the audience. Eventually, one man stood up and said, "As best I can tell, the only reason you want to put the prison here is for the jobs. Hell, we don't want any damn jobs. That's why we live in Martin County!" for which he received a nearly unanimous standing ovation. The private prison proposal was dead.

At Baker & Daniels, I also became involved in firm management. I was on the firm's management committee for five years, three as its chair, which was no mean feat for a lateral partner. I helped lead a strategic plan for the firm. We eschewed hiring a consulting firm, which I feared would just give us their generic "big law firm" product, and instead insisted on counseling with our clients as well as other business leaders (i.e., desired clients) as well as academics and other futurists. By doing so, I think we created a much better plan. One of the things that process and my tenure on the management committee taught me was that you can't cut your way to profitability. Although it's always important to keep an eye on expenses and to be as efficient as possible, the only real way to be robustly profitable is to grow the revenue pie.

I've often thought that although academic credentials are very important, they should be simply a baseline for recruiting lawyers who have also demonstrated tenacity, creativity, and an ability to manage several demanding matters at the same time. I declared it the scrappiness factor and for a while was successful in making it a formal evaluative factor in our recruiting process. Also while on the management committee, we dealt with a partner who was brilliant, had an expertise in a very hot area of the law, and was generating huge revenue for the firm. The problem was that he was a huge jerk. He ignored policies of the firm, hoarded work, and treated the staff badly. Eventually, after some wringing of hands, we did the right thing and fired him as a partner, a painful and difficult thing to do. Of course, it ended up being addition by subtraction, and our only regret was that we hadn't done it sooner. This is my favorite example of an organization understanding that "we are what we tolerate." If you accept bad behavior, that becomes who you are and can't be dismissed as just "Bill being Bill" or "Jane being Jane."

Thankfully, I was also involved in attracting some outstanding lawyers to Baker & Daniels as well, including my good friend former Republican state senator, lieutenant governor candidate, and state chairman Murray Clark. We worked on a number of matters together that benefited by having a high-profile Democrat and Republican on them. I also recruited Evan Bayh to join our firm after he left the governor's office, which I felt was a bit coming full circle from me having worked for his father's law firm in law school.

One of my most impactful experiences from serving on the management committee actually occurred during a break at one of our meetings. I had offhandedly shared with my partner Rich Hill that I had this bittersweet feeling that I was living what I would look back on as the good old days of life with my kids ranging in ages from around fourteen to five, and I was trying my best just to soak it up. Rich, who was quite a bit older than me, smiled, alluded to those being great ages, and encouraged me to "soak them up." But he also said, "You know, Fred, I just got back from a trip with my twenty-six-year-old son to see Van Morrison in Dublin, and it was the best time with him that I ever had." That hit me like a thunderbolt. Every age with your children is a great age. From almost that exact moment on, I became better at not wistfully looking back on bygone days when the kids were younger doing little-kid things and not eagerly (or dreadfully!) looking ahead to when they would be older doing bigger-kid things. Rather, I have just tried to enjoy them at every age. And Rich was right. Among the best times I've ever had as a parent are now as I interact with them as adults.

In my fifteen years at Baker & Daniels, the longest job I've ever had, I was able to build a practice from nothing to one of the most significant in the firm, resulting in me becoming among its most highly compensated partners. At the same time, perhaps not coincidentally, the firm provided me great flexibility and support to be a leader in the firm and my community. Becoming a lawyer gave me not only a distinguishing credential, but a special skill set, especially, as it was honed practicing at Baker & Daniels, of being able to communicate well both orally and in writing and, perhaps most useful of all, an ability to cut through the chaff of an issue to get to its wheat. And as we'll see in chapter 13, being a lawyer served me very well in pursuing and executing my role as the athletic director at Indiana University.

# 10. PRESIDENTIAL POLITICS

One of the ways I got off the beaten billable hours path at Baker &
was to agree to Evan's request that I serve as the Indiana chairmar
1996 Clinton-Gore presidential campaign. It was great working for
president as opposed to someone challenging an incumbent of tl
party or, even worse, one of many candidates chasing the nomin
their own party. Still, it was challenging and time-consuming, fo
ple, to secure the required congressional district-by-district signa
get the ticket officially on the ballot and put together a delegation
convention that met all the detailed diversity requirements of the r
party rules. We did it, and I had an incredible experience at the con
in Chicago. We ended up being a high-profile delegation because th
dent had selected Evan to be the convention's keynote speaker.

At the convention, Barbara and I were out late, like seeing-tl
come-up late, with friends enjoying some rare time away from our
tal responsibilities. George, our youngest, was only six months o
a couple of hours after we had gotten to bed, I got a call from the (
campaign offering to get me on the president's train that he was fai
taking into Chicago for the convention! I needed to leave right awa
on a plane for Michigan City to meet the train. Hmmm. On the one
be part of history and ride into Chicago with the president of the 1
States of America, on the other, nurse my stupendous hangover, g
to bed, and avoid having to fly (which I hate). I'm not proud to say I
the latter. I guess this is one where I did let an opportunity go by bec
didn't come at a convenient time. Shame on me!

I did have many other opportunities to meet President Clinton,
role as his Indiana campaign chair led to invitations for me and B;

to the 1996 Christmas parties at both the White House and the vice president's residence at the US Naval Observatory, as well as an invitation to the 1997 Fourth of July fireworks on the lawn of the White House, to which we were able also to bring all our kids, plus Mom and Aunt Miriam. The kids loved the free Dove Bars! As his Indiana campaign chair, I also received a special invitation for me and my family to attend Bill Clinton's second inauguration in 1997, including a variety of special events surrounding it. We took all four of the kids and stood out in the cold at a fairly decent spot to watch the president be sworn in. For most of us, it wasn't our first presidential inauguration. In 1993, while still serving as chief of staff, and with the good offices of Evan Bayh, who had gotten quite close to Bill Clinton, we also had good tickets to President Clinton's first inauguration. We had watched the new president be sworn in, minus only George, who had not yet been born.

My most meaningful visit with President Clinton had been at what turned out to be one of his infamous White House coffees, which were criticized by his opponents as inappropriate payoffs or influence peddling for his fat-cat donors. Of course, such criticism was a joke as applied to me and, as far as I could tell, to most of those attending with me, who seemed also to be more grassroots political activist types. In any event, our coffee was an early one, on January 24, 1996, the day after his State of the Union Address. When specifically asked by him for advice, I encouraged the president not to get too caught up in the perspectives and politics of Washington officeholders, pundits, and lobbyists, but to remember his political power came directly from the people. I told him that back in Indiana with Evan, we called that avoiding "limestone disease," that is, thinking everything important happened inside the limestone walls of the State House. He engaged me in the famous way he has with people and seemed to ponder my comments before saying, "Limestone disease. I like that. I'll remember that." I left the meeting feeling pretty good about myself.

As we departed the White House, a number of news photographers and videographers were around while we had our final goodbyes with the president. Much to my amusement, our departure—with me prominently visible in it—became CNN's B-roll that it would use almost every time it did a White House coffee story. A series of pictures captured from White House office videos, including one with me and President Clinton, even appeared in *Mad Magazine*. When my kids saw that I was actually in *Mad Magazine*, they felt I had finally made it.

Later, in 2009, right after I had been appointed IU's athletic director, I took Barbara, Connor, and George (Katie was working, and Joe was at

Marquette) to see the historic inauguration of Barack Obama. It was a wonderful, optimistic time. In the days leading up to the swearing in, everyone you would see and meet walking on and around the Mall was so excited. It was obviously particularly meaningful to the many African Americans who had come to DC for this special, unprecedented ceremony.

The night before the swearing in, as we had at our previous two inaugurations, Barbara and I attended the Indiana Society of Washington D.C. Dinner, which is a bipartisan gathering of Hoosiers hosted by the Indiana congressional delegation and chaired by an individual congressperson and his or her spouse. For this year, the chairs were Congressman Mike Pence and his wife, Karen. Barbara and I were the guests of my new employer, Indiana University, which was one of the primary event sponsors. We sat at its table at the front of the room near the stage with other senior IU administrators—most of whom were prominent Republicans—as well as President and First Lady McRobbie—liberal Democrats. Barbara had planned to drink only one glass of wine so as not to risk getting carried away in front of my new boss, his wife, and my new colleagues. The problem was that a very attentive waiter kept filling Barbara's wineglass before it was empty; her one glass ended up being somewhat more than that. With troops still in the field as part of the fallout of the Gulf War, Mrs. Pence introduced, one by one, a representative of every branch of the service, who then walked the length of the stage, saluted Mrs. Pence, and received the ongoing standing ovation from the crowd. Barbara, however, was putting her own little twist on the proceedings, yelling, "If you love 'em, bring 'em home! Bring 'em home!" and gesturing over her head for them to come on home. I certainly admired her perspective and enthusiasm.

DC hotel rooms were at a premium, and that night, Barbara, our two boys, and I, plus our close friends the O'Connor's family of five, all stayed in a single hotel room with one queen-sized bed. We laughed that we were the Beverly Hillbillies, but it was a great adventure to actually attend the swearing in of the first African American president of the United States. We got up very early the next day and took the subway to Capitol Hill. It was a madhouse. We had good tickets but couldn't get anywhere near our seats. The huge crowd apparently overwhelmed the event staff and police. There were no real lines.

There didn't seem to be anyone in charge. The cynic in me suspected that institutional racism had, unwittingly or not, left this substantially African American crowd to its own devices. In any event, it was out of control, and we eventually, reluctantly, concluded we wouldn't be able to get there.

We walked over to a commercial district on Constitution Avenue near Capitol Hill that I had enjoyed when I was an intern. Barbara and I and the boys, ours and the O'Connor's, went into a little Greek restaurant, empty but for the apparently first-generation American husband and wife owners. We watched in total silence Barack Obama's swearing in on a small black-and-white TV perched on top of their refrigerator. I noticed tears running down the cheeks of our hosts and suddenly felt less disappointed about not being there in person, as "in person" seemed to be in the eye of the beholder.

Joe Biden's swearing in as vice president was bittersweet, as he and Evan Bayh had seemed to have been the finalists to be Barack Obama's running mate. It had been eerie seeing on TV the press staking out Evan's house, a house Barbara and I had been in many times, as the decision grew near; unfortunately from our perspective, it went the other way. Shortly thereafter, Bart Peterson, John Dillon, and I decided to go out to DC to cheer Evan up. Evan is not a big drinker, but we sensed he was ready to cut loose a bit, and we were right. After a long night of drinking, Patron Tequila mostly, we took a cab to Evan's house to drop him off. I chivalrously walked him to his door, where we were met by his wonderful wife and my good friend, Susan, who looked none too happy. I greeted Susan, trying to summon up my most sober-sounding tone, but I think she saw through it, especially after I stumbled and rolled down the hill on their front lawn.

In our questionable states, Bart, John, and I thought it would be a good idea next to go to one of my favorite Capitol Hill bars, the Irish Times, for a few beers, and so we did. At one point, Bart said something to me to which I apparently took offense, and I looked him right in the eye while I poured a full beer on his crotch. Shortly thereafter, we all agreed that we should retire to our respective hotel rooms. The next day, Evan's assistant Christi called me and asked, "What did you guys do to him?" Mission accomplished.

# 11. SERVING A MAYOR

Bart Peterson became one of my closest friends as we worked together on Evan's first gubernatorial campaign and then served together in the governor's office. As previously discussed, upon my recommendation, he became Evan's deputy chief of staff while I was chief of staff and, later, my successor. Bart was always more of a policy wonk than a political guy, and although very funny and personable, he wasn't given to working a room like some of the future political candidates and officeholders in the Bayh administration. That is why I was shocked when he and Amy came over to our house and told me and Barbara that he was going to take on what seemed at the time as a longshot 1999 run to become the first Democrat elected Indianapolis mayor in thirty-six years. Later, on one of our annual trips to Green Bay, Bart told me he wanted me to drop him off at O'Hare Airport in Chicago on the way back, as he was going to fly to DC to solicit the critical support of the congresswoman from Indianapolis, Julia Carson. Although he had a general idea of the people he wanted to visit as he prepared for his mayoral run, he had no strategy of whom he would try to see when or in what sequence. He was just going to go see whom he could as their schedules allowed! This blew my anal-retentive mind. Not just because it ultimately worked, as he cleared a crowded primary field and defeated the establishment Republican candidate, but rather his approach taught me a practical lesson in the value of just getting out there and not overthinking things with the delay and disruption doing so creates. In short, it was a real-life application of the common admonition to avoid analysis paralysis.

Bart the businessman's approach was perhaps not surprisingly similar to that of one of my heroes, Bill Cook. Bill Cook, who with his wife,

Gayle, built the medical device company Cook Inc. from nothing to a multibillion-dollar enterprise, would eschew hiring consultants to evaluate and plan initiatives; he'd just start doing them, hence, the name of his biography by Bob Hammel, *The Bill Cook Story: Ready, Fire, Aim!*, based on one of his favorite maxims. He said he spent less and learned more by just jumping in and starting to implement his ideas in the real world rather than having them theoretically reviewed and evaluated in advance by consultants and other so-called experts. Nonetheless, planning is important, even while we recognize its limitations. Perhaps I adhere more to Dwight Eisenhower's admonition that "in preparing for battle I have always found that plans are useless, but planning is indispensable." Still, even if you have a plan, you can't wait for the elusive perfect time to move out. General George Patton was right: "A good plan immediately executed is better than a perfect plan executed next week."

Once late in August before the election, I said to mayoral candidate Bart, as I often did, "Hey, man, let me know if there is ever anything I can do for you."

At first, he just said thanks, but then he said, "You know, people say that to me all the time and that just becomes one more damn thing I have to do. I wish someone would just come and start doing stuff without me having to figure out what the hell it is!" In fairness, this was a very stressful point in any campaign. As crazy as he sounded, which candidates tend to do, I knew exactly what he meant. So I decided just to "be around" him and the campaign as much as possible between then and election day. I just showed up the next day and started riding around with him to events, helping out in the office, talking strategy, and sometimes just shooting the breeze and letting him be him. This is just another example of Woody Allen being right that 80 percent of success in life is just showing up. I'm so grateful that Bart felt comfortable enough with me to have his little outburst to make me realize that he just needed me to be present.

Bart was elected handily, and he asked me to chair his transition team, which I happily did. Even after the transition, I continued to be a regular advisor for him. Having helped recruit a great group of smart and talented, although largely inexperienced—with some significant exceptions—people to that staff, I felt it incumbent on me to accept Bart's request that I just "be around" to provide some "adult supervision." This role felt a lot like what I imagined being a grandfather would be like: coming over to the twenty-fifth floor and helping by listening and occasionally providing some counsel, but then leaving and returning to my real life. In that first term, John Dillon provided a similar function, although in the second term he formally joined the fray as Bart's chief of staff. At one of Bart's classic big meetings on a topic long since forgotten, with a conference table full of about twenty young staffers, John and I started getting into it pretty good over something or other. It must have gotten rather heated and loud because Bart's press secretary and our former colleague from the governor's office, Steve Campbell, felt compelled to say, "Hey, settle down, you guys. You're scaring the children."

Two major initiatives Bart undertook were fixing the combined sewer overflow (the disgusting practice of dumping sewage into the city's streams and rivers during heavy rains) and building the much-needed, centrally located new midfield terminal at the airport. Previous administrations had talked about these projects but had been unable to deliver them. In addition to being major accomplishments of the Peterson administration, these initiatives are good examples of how clear, consistent, positive communication is important to engendering public support. Words matter.

On the combined sewer overflow, Bart kept describing his three-part solution as a "three-legged stool." I told him it wasn't a good idea to talk about fixing the problem of poop in rivers by referencing a "stool." Bart's good with words too. At his press conference announcing his resolution to the combined sewer overflow problem, he opened by saying, "If loving sewers is wrong, I don't want to be right."

I also challenged him on why he kept referring to a midfield terminal. Yes, to engineers and airport executives, we were talking about a new arrival and departure building in the middle of the airfield, a "midfield terminal." But for the public, who didn't care that the runways and everything else would be the same, this magnificent building would be the "new Indianapolis Airport," a bigger point of pride for both Indianapolis and the Peterson administration than a "midfield terminal." Therefore, Bart and his staff, and ultimately the media, always referred to the project as the new Indianapolis Airport, which Bart was able to build and has continued to win award after award.

Of course, Bart's job was one of high stress, and he went all-out all the time. He could get himself worked up. I remember one stressful meeting where he threw his hands up in the air and said, "This is crazy. I don't have time for anything. You could tell me that the president of the United States of America is on the phone and I'd have to say, 'I'm sorry, I'm just too busy to talk to him right now.'"

Every once in a while, I took it upon myself to try to get him to relax and have some fun. It was a tough duty, but somebody had to do it. For example, in the heat of the Colts negotiations, I was having trouble getting on his schedule to brief him on recent developments and get his direction, which I needed to do in advance of a major meeting we were going to have with our broader team on the subject. He kept putting it off, telling me he was overscheduled with no available time. I finally said the night before the team meeting, "Look, you have to eat. Let's grab a quick dinner and go over this stuff." He reluctantly agreed to give me forty-five minutes. We met at the Claddagh Irish Pub downtown and very quickly dealt with the business at hand before getting heavy into the Irish whiskeys. Apparently, I had been feeling a little stressed too. Luckily, his security person took each of us home. Our fellow attendees at the meeting the next day were rather disappointed with us because we were feeling a little hurt and having trouble concentrating and not giggling.

* * *

Although during the transition I never expected to have a formal position with the administration, Bart asked me to serve on the Marion County Capital Improvement Board of Managers, the CIB, essentially the local stadium authority controlling the home of the NFL Indianapolis Colts, NBA Indianapolis Pacers, Minor League Baseball Indianapolis Indians, as well as the Indiana Convention Center. With the support of the other newly appointed members, as well as the holdover Republican members who understood the mayor should be able to choose this important body's leadership, I was elected its president at my first meeting. I asked prominent Republican holdover Pat Early, who had been president for the previous eight years, to serve as my vice president, knowing that any substantial initiatives would have to have bipartisan support given that the City-County Council and both houses of the Indiana General Assembly were controlled by Republicans. Importantly, I trusted Pat, who was a political pro, loved the city, and was a close friend of my pal John Dillon. Pat was a great partner who helped us get big things done and never breached our trust.

The biggest challenge facing the CIB, and arguably the entire administration, was the very real prospect of Indianapolis losing the NFL Colts. The previous administration had entered into an agreement with the team that added a few more years to the lease by guaranteeing that the team would be at the median in NFL revenues, which we estimated could require an annual subsidy of $14 million. Even if the city could afford such payments, which it couldn't, making them would be not only costly, but stupidly futile, since it would just be delaying the team's fairly soon likely departure.

Our vision for saving the Colts was to build a new multiuse stadium, what would ultimately become Lucas Oil Stadium. Instead of subsidizing the Colts to the tune of tens of millions of dollars to stay just a few more years under the terms of their then-current lease, we wanted a new long-term lease, with no guaranties to the team, made possible by the revenues that could be generated by a new stadium. A new stadium would also enable us to seize some other opportunities. First, we would be able to host additional Final Fours, which were at significant risk given that the NCAA had advised us that Indianapolis wouldn't be awarded any more unless the current RCA Dome was substantially upgraded or replaced. Second, a new stadium would enable us to substantially expand the convention center and thereby save and grow our lucrative hospitality industry by replacing the existing RCA Dome, which was sitting on the only feasible location for such a major expansion.

While we were confident that a new stadium was the answer, along with the convention center expansion it would make possible, we also understood this would constitute a historic and hugely expensive public-works project that would need the public's support. Therefore, not unlike with the combined sewer overflow and new Indianapolis Airport, we set about communicating clearly and consistently how the stadium would provide things that Indianapolis area residents care about: the Colts, Final Fours, jobs, and the quality of life enhanced by bars, restaurants, and the like made possible by the hospitality industry.

Our most immediate challenge was that the Colts weren't particularly interested in a new stadium; they liked their current deal based on the lucrative city subsidy payments. They were presumably and understandably content to collect them until the end of the lease and then entertain offers for the future location of the team. Given that at that point Indianapolis would have no stadium and would have wasted tens of millions of dollars to subsidize the team for the last few years of its lease, it is highly unlikely that we would have been in a position to successfully compete to keep the team. We were thus in the exact reverse situation of most NFL cities; it is usually the team wanting a new stadium and the city resisting. Indianapolis needed the new stadium to support its economy, quality of life, jobs, NCAA relationship, and status as an NFL city, but the key was getting the Colts interested in the idea of a new stadium-based, long-term lease.

We concluded that the best way to do that was to get them to fall in love with the design of a new stadium. Toward that end, we asked four architectural firms to develop designs for a potential new stadium. As the key constituents for a new multipurpose stadium, we brought to the table to help draft its specs the Colts, the NCAA, and the Indianapolis Convention and Visitors Association (ICVA)—since we anticipated the new stadium to be physically connected to the expanded convention center and wanted its floor to be compatible as auxiliary convention and trade show space. Our vision was to design the new building specifically for those various uses and constituencies, rather than designed as a football stadium then backfilled for other uses. Unfortunately, the only locally based firm didn't participate, reportedly because it had heard we had already settled on selecting the industry leader in stadium design. Ironically, we did not select that firm but rather a new, as yet largely unproven, upstart stadium design firm, HKS. They designed an incredibly functional yet beautiful building reminiscent of a basketball fieldhouse, which, magnificent in its scale and impact, felt very much at home in the capital of this basketball-mad state. Hungry HKS listened to what we wanted. Although they were certainly the riskier choice, their professional, collaborative approach had won our confidence. Still, in the end, all that really mattered was that its design had captured the Colts' imagination and they were willing to negotiate a new deal based on that stadium design.

These are challenging negotiations, especially for small-market cities, because the teams have all the leverage. If they don't like the deal, they can walk away and almost certainly relocate to a city they perceive as a better market. Most cities that called its NFL team's bluff, telling the owner that the cost of keeping the NFL franchise was too high and letting their team go, have ended up paying even more to get a new franchise: St. Louis, Houston, Cleveland, and Baltimore, for example.

We believed it was particularly critical to keep the Colts in Indianapolis; if they left, unlike those other cities, we would never get another team. Mayor Hudnut's courageous and visionary gamble to essentially build what became the RCA Dome before he had an NFL team to play in it paid off when the Baltimore Colts moved to Indianapolis in 1984. That, however, was a historical accident the NFL wasn't going to let happen again. If the NFL had its way, the Colts wouldn't be in Indianapolis, smack dab in the middle of the markets of several other teams. We believed, fair or not, having an NFL team—more so than any other single attribute—makes you a "major league city." This is not only important to civic pride, but it can be important for economic development. It is a fact that being an NFL city is on the lists of some companies' relocation criteria. Importantly, it is part of the quality of life for a community not only for the fans of the team but for the hospitality amenities it helps support just by its presence. Moreover, in this era of multiple TV channels and news outlets, on-demand TV streaming, and social media and the internet, there are very few things that draw a community together—rich and poor, Black and White, etc.—like the local NFL team. So as a small market, we entered into conversations with the Colts for a long-term, stadium-based deal knowing that it was going to require substantial government support.

Our main goal was to get off the current lease, which allowed the Colts just to sit back and collect ever-increasing revenue subsidy checks consistent with ever-increasing NFL revenues, and move to a model where the Colts were at risk, without any city guaranty, for its revenue generation from a new stadium. After months of negotiations with the Colts, we were finally able to agree on a new thirty-year lease contingent on the new stadium being built. In essence, the city committed to build the stadium, with a $100 million contribution from the Colts, and retain ownership and operational control of it as the landlord but make the Colts a preferred tenant for a term of thirty years. The Colts would keep the revenues generated from Colts games—and some non-Colt events—but importantly without any guaranteed revenue.

The next trick was how to pay for it. I counseled with Pat Early about how he had led the effort to build and finance the new Pacers arena when he was CIB president. Although nowhere near the scope of this project not only to build a much more costly multiuse stadium but also dramatically expand the convention center, the new Pacers arena had been a challenging project in its own right. Pat rhetorically asked me, "How do you eat an elephant?" and then answered his own question: "One bite at a time." He went on to say, "If you look at the whole thing, you will be overwhelmed. Just start stacking revenue streams on each other." While simple advice, that was great advice, and that's just what we did.

Frustratingly, the duly elected mayor and City-County Council of Marion County could not, as a matter of state law, raise taxes or user fees in their own county without permission from the Republican-controlled General Assembly and, by extension, newly elected Republican governor. Although a strong philosophical argument could be made that we shouldn't have had to in the first place, we believed the only way to get that permission was to create overwhelming political pressure on them to give it by making it clear to the public that if the state didn't act then, it, not the city, would be to blame for "losing the Colts." That is why it was so important for us to get an agreement with the Colts on a new lease and put together a proposed funding package for the project before the legislative session started. Doing so effectively put the ball in the state's court. In the end, consistent with the constant private requests from the governor's staff and Republican legislative leaders to me that we "turn down the rhetoric,"

I am convinced that this pressure we put on the state not to be perceived as losing the Colts is why they ultimately acted. Thankfully, with Peyton Manning at the helm, the Colts were riding high, and no politician wanted to be blamed for losing them. That is why Lucas Oil Stadium is often fairly referred to as "the house that Peyton Built."

We started that process by dramatically announcing at halftime of a Sunday night football game, right before the start of the General Assembly's legislative session, that we had reached a deal with the Colts. The owner of the Colts, the head of the NCAA, the leaders of the ICVA, the mayor, and I triumphantly walked out to midfield holding hands with our arms raised at the old RCA Dome while the videoboard showed a 3D design video of the beautiful new stadium over Hoosier John Mellencamp's song "Check It Out," which I had selected, overruling some recommended crazy European techno-music. When the video showed the retractable roof opening, the crowd went nuts! It was outstanding political theater and helped put the onus of funding the stadium, or, more accurately, allowing Indianapolis to fund the stadium and thus keeping the Colts, right where it had to be: on the state.

The next day, Bart and I held a press conference where we publicly detailed every element of the agreement we had reached with the Colts on behalf of the city. This was not only the right thing to do but the smart thing to do; subsequently, no legislator or reporter could credibly say we hid the ball on what was in the agreement. We stayed and answered every question until there were no more. I followed that with an op-ed column in the *Indianapolis Star* also detailing every significant element of the deal, both the terms favorable to the city that we wanted *and* the terms favorable to the Colts that we had to give to get what we wanted. Many times in the sojourn to get final approvals and funding for the stadium did I refer back to that press conference and editorial to prove that we had been transparent on all the terms, including whatever element some deal critic had latched on to and inaccurately claimed that we had hidden.

Being completely transparent about the good, the bad, and especially the ugly of our deal stole a lot of the power of its potential critics to unearth the flaws. I had learned the value of this early self-reporting transparency in 1988. Evan's opponent in the governor's race, well-respected Lieutenant Governor John Mutz, had spearheaded an economic development deal to bring a Subaru-Isuzu manufacturing plant to Indiana, which seemed like a huge political victory for him. He ballyhooed it, focusing exclusively on the positives and minimizing or ignoring many of the "gives" that the state understandably had to make to get the deal done. As an advisor to the campaign on economic development, among other, issues I was asked to dig into the deal to see if there were any issues with it that might be pointed out and criticized by Evan. There were several, which he attacked with some gusto. They even made their way into a number of television commercials many credit with helping him win the election. I believe a great deal of the power of this criticism came from the fact that Lieutenant Governor Mutz hadn't disclosed these issues himself on the front end and, in fact, had made some representations that were inconsistent with the deal's true terms. Had he accurately set out the "gives" he made to get the "gets" up front, we would have been denied the more dramatic impact of finding them out and exposing them, and I think our criticism would have been much less powerful. That's why I was so determined, over the objections of some (not Bart, who had also lived 1988), to be the first to transparently detail the entire deal, warts and all.

We were always prepared to fund the stadium and convention center expansion primarily though Marion County resources, such as increases to the Marion County innkeepers, auto rental excise, and admission taxes, which often are paid with income from nonresidents or others who choose to use the services or venues being taxed. Importantly, we were completely opposed to using Marion County property, sales, or income taxes, which we felt would be an undue burden on Marion County residents. A central feature of our proposed funding package centered on tax revenues that would be generated from a new downtown Indianapolis casino, the ultimate user/chooser fee, which many of us believed would complement and help grow our hospitality industry. Even though we thought it highly likely that the General Assembly would reject the casino idea, it was critical for us to have a proposal for funding the entire project so that the General Assembly couldn't credibly claim that we were simply coming hat in hand for them to solve our problems. We were in the positive situation of having a financial plan and being able to say, "We have a funding plan. If you don't like it, come up with your own or lose the Colts."

Ironically, one of the opponents to a downtown Indianapolis casino was Mayor Peterson himself. It took quite a bit of convincing and subsequent reinforcement to get him to support proposing the casino and the funding it could provide the stadium / convention center project so that we could have our own funding proposal to hit that issue back into the General Assembly's court. I think the only reason Bart supported it is because he believed it would fail and the General Assembly would have to come up with something else, most probably a series of Marion County taxes and user fees, which we were prepared to accept. Early on, the Republican legislative leadership, as we had expected, declared the casino proposal "dead on arrival," and it stayed that way. Bart was relieved. Politics is a crazy world, isn't it?

The Colts, the ICVA, and the NCAA were natural, and critical, allies in pursuing legislative approval for the stadium and expanded convention center. The Colts enjoyed strong relationships in the legislature, particularly in light of the popularity of the team and its players given their on-field success. To bolster our case, we commissioned a PricewaterhouseCoopers study of the economic impact of the stadium / convention center project, which found that not only Marion County, but its surrounding counties and the state as a whole, would greatly benefit financially from the project through additional jobs and other economic activity as well as increased tax revenues. The ICVA's powerful board members and the owners of its member hotels had loud voices at the Republican-controlled General Assembly. In addition to focusing on the need for the stadium to save the Colts, we aggressively campaigned on the need for an expanded convention center to preserve and strengthen the city's hospitality industry and the jobs and entertainment/lodging/restaurant facilities it made possible (which, PS, most of the out-of-town legislators loved to enjoy). We mobilized the hotel and restaurant workers to attend, en masse, pertinent hearings and otherwise work the State House, wearing their doorman, chef, maid, valet, maintenance, waiter, waitress, and other uniforms to help get our point across that this legislation was for more than the Colts but for economic development and jobs. A final big ace in the hole for us was that we were also accurately able to tie this project to a regular rotation of NCAA Final Fours. In basketball-crazed Indiana, this was a particularly popular public component of the overall arrangement. We worked that piece hard with individual legislators.

In the end, our message of keeping the Colts, securing Final Fours, and saving hospitality jobs resonated with legislators and gave them cover back home for giving Indianapolis the great privilege of taxing itself to provide this regional, or even statewide, benefit. Although Republicans controlled the governor's office and both houses of the General Assembly, as the legislative session wore on, I felt that the strength and benefits of our project, along with the public support and pressure we had been able to develop, would provide a successful result. It did too. Just not the way we had planned.

\* \* \*

Through most of the session, while negotiations among the legislative leadership, the governor's representatives, and us were sometimes contentious because of understandable competing interests, I always felt they were fairly transparent and marked by good faith. In many ways, it felt as though we were working together, like a team pursuing a common goal. We shared information. Talked strategy. Worked with our respective constituents, all of whom we would need if we were going to be successful. Then suddenly, late in the session, Governor Daniels told Bart that the only way he would support the project would be if the state took control of building the stadium and the convention center away from the CIB and the city of Indianapolis.

In his first conversation with Bart, he raised the subject rather sheepishly, almost unwillingly, but thereafter he was always resolute and unapologetic. He demanded the state control the construction, notwithstanding that no state entity existed for that purpose and that a Republican-controlled CIB had built every capital improvement in Indianapolis through its entire history, including the last major CIB capital improvement, the new Pacers arena. That building had been built by a Republican mayor and Republican-controlled CIB with the active support of Democratic governor Frank O'Bannon.

I did, and do, respect and admire Mitch Daniels. He is smart, practical, and innovative and wants to get big, important things done. I also like him personally, as he is interesting, funny, and engaging. In fact, subsequent to the stadium / convention center legislation and its related issues, I feel I've enjoyed a quite cordial relationship with him and was the beneficiary of his enthusiastic and effective support of the Indianapolis Super Bowl bid. I appreciate how he expressly eschewed exploiting divisive social/ wedge issues while he was governor. That's why his decision to take from Indianapolis the stadium / convention center project and, even worse, the CIB's money to ultimately operate and maintain those buildings was so unexpected and disappointing. It was unprecedented, unjustified, and gratuitously disparaging.

Among other things, Governor Daniels sought to justify the state takeover on the modest funding authority from surrounding counties that he had secured from the Republican-controlled state legislature. This regional contribution authority was certainly very significant symbolically and warranted as a matter of policy given the fiscal, quality of life, and other benefits the suburbs would enjoy from this project, as they do with many other Marion County–funded amenities they do not financially support. Thus, Governor Daniels deserves credit for leading the effort to secure it and perhaps even more so for subsequently personally advocating for the actual enactment of that contribution in the counties themselves. Still, the vast majority of the public funding in the project was coming from taxes being paid in Marion County. The comparatively very modest regional contribution certainly did not justify a forty-year break with tradition to have the state build a Marion County capital improvement. What changed? The politics of Marion County. When Republicans controlled Indianapolis, State House Republicans (and Democrats) were fine to support the city building its own capital improvements. It was only when Democrats won the mayor's office that the state decided it should build them instead of the city.

To add insult to injury, while the city's financing plan had always contemplated that the operation and maintenance costs of the new venues would be paid from the revenue streams also created for their design and construction, as had been done on most every major sports and hospitality project the city had ever previously undertaken and as is common around the country for major public infrastructure projects (specifically including professional sports stadiums), the state not only demanded control of building the project, but also the funds Indianapolis needed to operate and maintain those facilities. Worse than taking the project in the first place was taking it and then giving it back without the money to operate it. The state claimed it was doing so to pay off the project bonds sooner than required, but I and others—including, for example, IU professor Sheila Kennedy in a May 11, 2009, *Indianapolis Star* guest column retrospective—always have suspected the real intent was to bankrupt the CIB and then use that as a political weapon against Bart, who at the time was the strongest Democratic officeholder in the state and thus the biggest threat to the Republican political establishment.

Our concerns with the state's takeover of constructing the project and taking the funds that the city would need to operate and maintain the project were in addition to our concern that shifting control of the project from one entity to another this late in the game would inherently, unnecessarily, and dramatically increase the cost of the project. The nonpartisan executive director of the CIB, who was actually a holdover from previous Republican administrations, estimated that the extra cost to the project due to the state taking it over exceeded $25 million.

The mayor offered a number of compromises, even including adding the state inspector general and state budget director to the CIB (given the governor's claimed concerns about waste and mismanagement), which would have been the first state representation ever on that historically and statutorily local entity, but they were all rejected. In the end, over our strong protestations, Governor Daniels maintained his demand for state control of Indianapolis's stadium construction and convention center expansion and the funds necessary to operate and maintain them. It became clear that in order to save our baby, we were going to have to give it away. And that's exactly what Bart did with seven days left in the legislative session on April 22, 2005, in an act of great political courage and magnanimity. In a press release appropriately titled "Mayor ends stadium stalemate to move project forward; Peterson breaks with 30-year tradition, turns local project over to state," the mayor described the governor's control demand as "a bolt out of the blue" that he continued to disagree with. Still, he stated that "this project—and the thousands of jobs and the $2.25 billion of economic benefit to Indianapolis—is too important to Indianapolis to let the project remain at a standstill."

The mayor's acquiescence to state control expressly included some reasonable conditions, including that contracts for the project would be awarded by a nonpolitical process; an adequate minority- and women-owned-business participation requirement would be in place; and, perhaps most importantly, the CIB would receive the newly authorized revenues to help pay debt service and operations and maintenance for the project. For the remainder of the session, the city continued to push publicly and privately the need to include funding for operation and maintenance in the state legislation and funding plan. Through an *Indianapolis Star* article published April 27, I purposefully pointed out publicly that "the State's plan does not include money to run the stadium and 'will bankrupt' the board." Given my inability to persuade state leaders to acknowledge and address this issue, I had gone to the reporter's office to make my case and specifically give him that quote. In the end, Governor Daniels and Republican state legislative leaders refused to reconsider taking Indianapolis's operation and maintenance funds along with the construction of the stadium and convention center.

\* \* \*

Meanwhile, Governor Daniels and his staff, as well as Republican legislative leaders, were having a hard time getting the votes for passage, even though they had gotten exactly what they demanded. Gubernatorial staffers and Republican legislative leaders were privately calling me, asking to help get them Democratic votes even though their party comfortably controlled both houses of the General Assembly. The day the legislature was to adjourn, what the *Indianapolis Star* described as "an angry Governor Mitch Daniels" said to an *Indianapolis Star* reporter, "Your stadium is about to go down." He also acknowledged for the article that he called

Mayor Peterson to talk about the project. I was there when he did so. He not only asked Bart to help him get votes for his legislation, but he went on to describe what great people would be on the new state authority, not realizing—or perhaps caring—what an insult that was to the members of the Indianapolis CIB whose authority he was attempting to displace. While the governor was asking Bart to help him get Democratic legislator votes, particularly from Indianapolis and Lake County, he was also suggesting, as reflected in the article, that Indianapolis and Lake County couldn't be trusted to make wise decisions and spend public money well and honestly. My daughter, who was a student at IU at the time, read these quotes and emailed me to ask me why the governor of Indiana was saying this about me. She encouraged me to hang in there. Although I was pleased with her attempt to comfort me, it was upsetting that she had been put in a position to feel the need to.

In the article, the governor also called for publicly what he and his allies had been insisting on privately, that Indianapolis quit "demanding more" because we were already "getting 98 percent of everything that [we] asked for." Beyond being an almost humorous comment in light of our historic ceding of control of the project to the state, the remaining "2 percent" that we felt we justifiably needed was not only critical to attracting Democratic votes but critical to the success of the project as well, even though the governor dismissed it in the article as "minutia." We believed to attract Democratic votes and to better the project, we especially needed the operation and maintenance funding that was always included in such projects. "The governor is done talking terms" is all the governor's staff and Republican legislative leaders would say to me.

* * *

In the end, Bart personally went to the House Democratic caucus and asked them to set aside the bill's imperfections and slights and vote for it for the people of Indianapolis. Bart had already saved the project once by acceding to the governor's demand that he and the state control the project. Although we continued to be particularly concerned about the state commandeering the project's operation and maintenance funding, we believed that getting the project done for Indianapolis was bigger than all the concerns and that there was enough funding to fix the operation and maintenance issue if cooler heads could later prevail. There was strong sentiment among many Democratic legislators, especially those from Marion and Lake Counties, simply to vote against what they viewed as unfair and flawed legislation, particularly given the inflammatory rhetoric from the governor. But to his great credit, Bart asked them to vote for the bill: "No one understands your frustration more than me nor the injustice of having to not only accept this insult but to facilitate it, but the stakes for our community and region are too high, so I ask you to give them the votes they need." It was a moment worthy of a chapter in *Profiles in Courage*. With bittersweet bemusement, Bart watched from the House gallery as the stadium / convention center legislation passed an hour before midnight on April 29, 2005, the last day of the legislative session. It wasn't how we had drawn it up on the chalkboard, but it had gotten done. The Colts were saved, Final Fours secured, the convention center expanded, the hospitality industry invigorated, and a Super Bowl would be hosted.

* * *

Bart and I have cottages near each other in Northern Michigan. It's not a coincidence. When Bart was looking for a cottage in the swankier area of Saugatuck, Michigan, I suggested he look much farther north, near my cottage in the decidedly less swanky Mackinaw City area, where he could get more house and be on Lake Michigan for much less money. He and Amy were skeptical, but they came up to visit one weekend and left having made an offer on a cottage by ours. In any event, in the fall of 2006, we drove up north together to stay at our places and spend a weekend talking about whether he should run for a third term in the fall of 2007. On the way up, I had strongly sensed he had made up his mind not to run, and although I was disappointed for the city of Indianapolis, he was my friend first; I didn't try to talk him out of it.

Mostly over beers, we talked all weekend about the pros and cons. Being an activist, engaged mayor takes it out of you. I was, and am, proud to be associated with him. He took on challenges at great political risk to get important things done. He'd successfully pushed for Lucas Oil Stadium and a major expansion of the Indiana Convention Center to save the Colts, Final Fours, and Indianapolis's hospitality industry; the new Indianapolis Airport; fixing the combined sewer overflow problem; neighborhood renovations like Fall Creek Place; education reform through charter schools; the cultural trail; and many other achievements. We were also in the midst of planning for a bid for Indianapolis to host a Super Bowl. At the same time, Bart had been worn down by unsuccessful fights with the Indiana General Assembly to modernize and streamline the city's anachronistic township government and, as with most mayors, by a contentious relationship with the police union. That challenge was behind a ruthless personal campaign by some police officers and their supporters against the mayor, including having a costumed guy with his face covered follow him around with a sign that read "Bart Lies." The goof even went to the effort to have his picture taken in his getup in front of my cottage in Northern Michigan, thinking it was Bart's. This was particularly upsetting to Barbara and gave us some sense of how personal and violative this type of stuff must have been for Bart and Amy.

Bart felt heavily and personally every murder during a nationwide surge in murders from which Indianapolis was not immune. He was present at everything. Neighborhood meetings. Ethnic festivals. Parades. Comforting crime victims. Police roll calls. After nearly eight years, my friend was tired. The more we talked, the more I became convinced that he wasn't going to run again. And then we drove home. He was trying his decision not to run on for size, and it didn't seem to fit. He had more he wanted to do, especially in battling crime. As I look back, maybe more than anything else, he just didn't want to be a quitter. In any event, by the time we got home, it was clear to me he was going to run for a third term.

Bart was popular, and no prominent Republican wanted to challenge him. He ended up running by default against Greg Ballard, who had held administrative positions in the Marine Corps, and, commendably, over twenty-three years rose to the rank of lieutenant colonel before retiring. After that he was a self-employed leadership and management consultant and taught seminars at the for-profit Indiana Business College. He self-published a book called *The Ballard Rules: Small Unit Leadership.* Barbara had grown up near him, and their brothers were best friends. We would see him on the campaign trail, and he was always just standing around by himself. We often were the only ones who would talk to him. It looked like Bart was going to kill him. Then not long before the election, a property tax crisis hit the state, including Indianapolis. While it was a statewide crisis allowed to happen by state policymakers, mayors were closest to the angry property owners and the next ones up for election, and they paid the political price. Moreover, while Bart knew that the property tax issue made his race a much tougher one, he courageously decided to pursue a 0.1 percent increase in the local option income tax to help support the severely underfunded police officer pension to free up more operational dollars to fight crime.

Ballard rode the property tax fiasco anger and his opposition to the tax increase, most of which he later happily spent on things other than fighting crime, to victory. Ironically, that no one knew who he was and that he had no record or platform to run on played to his benefit, as his campaign was essentially one of "none of the above." His own campaign signs didn't mention his name but rhetorically asked, "Had enough?" Voters mad about their property taxes skyrocketing and wanting someone to blame, blamed Bart even though it wasn't his fault. Yet another *Profiles in Courage* moment to raise the income tax in the face of voter anger over the property tax to fight crime didn't help either. Although I was disappointed for Bart and the city of Indianapolis, I was proud he went down swinging, fighting for what he believed in and what was right.

I came in with Bart, and I would go out with him as well. That's how it should work. I always understood that I had my roles with the city because I was Bart's guy and he had confidence in me, not because I had some special mastery of, or entitlement to, them. I announced the Monday after the election that I would resign from the CIB at the end of that calendar year, coinciding with the end of Bart's term. As reflected in an *Indianapolis Star* article about my resignation, Ballard had made it clear to me that he wanted me to stay, but I felt strongly that he should be able to pick his own person:

> The decision came as a surprise to Republican Mayor-elect Greg Ballard. "I was not expecting it, and I did not ask for it," Ballard said. "I was hoping he'd hang on." Glass said that's exactly what he didn't want to do. "I became president of my first meeting because I was Mayor Peterson's guy, and I think the new mayor ought to have that same opportunity," he said. "I wanted to clear the deck and make sure there was no misunderstanding that I was going to somehow claw on and stay on. I like to think that's not my style. I had my chance, and now it's time for somebody else to." (November 12, 2007)

I didn't take my ball and go home. Rather, I worked with the new mayor and his team to facilitate the best transition possible. This included comprehensive, transparent briefings on all CIB issues, including a detailed transition letter I sent to Mayor-elect Ballard's transition team on December 18, 2007, describing the three major issues I suggested merited the most attention: "the completion of the stadium/convention center project; the CIB's future cash flow position as impacted by the state's failure to fund the new stadium's operation and maintenance needs; and the potential reopening of the Pacers/Conseco Fieldhouse Lease Agreement." When you go out, go out the right way.

This major disappointment for Bart and the people closest to him, including me, ended up being a huge blessing in disguise for us all. Sound familiar? Bart became a senior executive at local pharmaceutical giant Eli Lilly, where he had a distinguished and lucrative career, and later CEO of Christel House International, which uses a holistic model to educate and improve the lives of children around the world. Our longtime colleague John Dillon, who had served as Bart's chief of staff, went on to be the president of his own insurance company. Chief Counsel Keira Amstutz, who had been one of Bart's first campaign staffers, became the very highly respected president of Indiana Humanities. Press Secretary Steve Campbell became vice president of communications for his beloved Indianapolis Colts. The list of "Peterson people" landing on their feet goes on and on.

It was true for me as well. If Bart had won and I was still serving as president of the CIB, I never would have abandoned him and his pursuit of the Super Bowl and a successfully completed Lucas Oil Stadium to become the athletic director at IU. So although I firmly believe Bart's defeat was bad for the city of Indianapolis, it worked out well for Bart and me personally, as well as others closest to him. Our greatest disappointments can create our greatest opportunities if we don't let them deter us.

It is no doubt harder for Bart to similarly embrace this karma. I've been as close to it as you can be more times than I like, but I can't know how hard it must be personally to have your name on the ballot and lose, even if for the wrong reasons outside of your control and even if losing leads to better things for you personally. Thus, he found little humor in my later suggestions that he name Amy's delightful home goods store as well as the beautiful boat he bought *Third Term*.

# 12. BRINGING THE SUPER BOWL TO INDY

We had always been very careful in our public and legislative pursuit of what became Lucas Oil Stadium never to promise that it would result in Indianapolis hosting a Super Bowl. I publicly described it as the cherry on the sundae of the new stadium, expanded convention center, keeping the Colts, guaranteeing Final Fours, and saving the hospitality industry. Still, we were determined to get that cherry. Pursuing a Super Bowl as a host is one of the most complicated and competitive exercises a city will ever undertake. Once we had the authority and funding in place to build the new stadium, our attention turned toward pursuing a Super Bowl with the next available opportunity in 2011.

\* \* \*

Early in 2006, while I was still at Baker & Daniels and serving as the volunteer president of Indianapolis's stadium authority, Mayor Peterson asked me to come up with a list of names of people who would be capable of leading a successful effort to pursue hosting the Super Bowl in Indianapolis. He and I met along with Keira Amstutz, Steve Campbell, and our mutual confidant John Dillon in a private room for lunch at Dunaway's in the old Oxygen Company to discuss the list and try to choose someone to ask to do it. After reviewing my list and discussing the pros and cons of those on it, I had to excuse myself to go to the bathroom. When I got back, they were all just sitting there smiling at me. "We're unanimous," Bart said. "It needs to be you." I was shocked. My name wasn't on the list!

I really didn't want to do it. I felt that I had way too much to do staying engaged in the stadium project, trying to protect the city's interests as the state built a stadium the city would be expected to operate. Also, truth be told, I questioned whether I had the chops to lead such an important and public initiative that would require taking a high profile, something I had never really done before. I met with Bart privately to tell him I was turning down his flattering suggestion, but Bart wouldn't take no for an answer. He told me: "Look, you're just playing defense now. That's no fun. Here's a chance for you to have some fun and play some offense." I agreed to do it. Accept opportunities presented to you even if you're not sure you are ready or even capable, because all that matters is that the person offering you the opportunity believes you are.

*  *  *

From the beginning, Bart and I were committed to going all-out for the Super Bowl. We believed that beyond the economic impact and international media exposure for Indianapolis, landing the Super Bowl would also be a huge confidence builder for the city. Bereft of natural assets like a seashore, mountains, or even a navigable river, Indianapolis had built itself into a thriving city through visionary leadership and can-do civic pride and activism. For those same reasons and more, however, securing the Super Bowl would be particularly valuable to Indianapolis. Many in the city still suffering from an inferiority complex thought that Indianapolis just wasn't Super Bowl material, which made the benefits of succeeding all the more attractive. We are a great event city, and we knew if we got the chance, we would set a new standard. Indianapolis was built for hosting events, famously, yes, for Final Fours, but also less famously—but even more importantly—for huge conventions and trade shows. As the current stewards of Indianapolis and its can-do civic and governmental tradition, we believed it to be our duty for the people who had elected Bart mayor. By hosting a great Super Bowl, we hoped to become less of the bittersweet "great little secret" that visitors would often declare of Indianapolis. We looked forward to being able to tell the National Optometric Association, by random example, that we can host the Super Bowl of optometrist conventions because we had successfully hosted the actual Super Bowl! Seize every opportunity to the fullest. Own it. Exceed expectations. Confirm the confidence that has been placed in you and show that you are capable of even more.

Deciding to very publicly and aggressively pursue the Super Bowl is just another example of Bart Peterson eschewing the politically safe course to pursue important, but risky, initiatives that other politicians might have avoided. This was especially true as to the Super Bowl effort, which was being pursued in an election year. Bart's opponent, Greg Ballard, very publicly and aggressively opposed pursuing the Super Bowl, saying that we shouldn't do so until the crime problem was fixed. That his position was the worst form of craven political opportunism was confirmed when right after he was elected mayor, he supported the Super Bowl bid even though, of course, he hadn't fixed the crime problem—and never did.

Although winning a bid to host the Super Bowl was far from a foregone conclusion, I always believed we could do it and would do it through the creativity and hard work that has been a hallmark for our city. I thought it was important to lead with that confidence. The *Indianapolis Star* made this observation:

> Glass still is surprised to hear some people tell him there's no chance Indianapolis will land the Super Bowl. It's a city with a history of betting on the come. The Colts wouldn't be here if the city didn't build the Hoosier Dome first. The NCAA headquarters wouldn't be here if the business and political leaders didn't muster the money and effort. "I thought we had rubbed that out," Glass said of the naysayers. "One of the benefits when we do win this will be that it's a reaffirmation of what we can do when we toss our hat over the wall." Now that's confidence. (April 3, 2007)

My public confidence notwithstanding, which I hoped would become a self-fulfilling prophecy, I knew we had our work cut out for us. Only two northern cities had ever hosted the game before (Minneapolis and Detroit), and very few other small markets had ever done so. Atlanta—not a northern city but also not one of the traditional Super Bowl resort cities (Miami, New Orleans, and Los Angeles have hosted twenty-eight Super Bowls)—had just recently hosted one of the most criticized Super Bowls ever because of an unusual ice storm that gripped the city, which wasn't prepared to handle it. Our competition for the 2011 Super Bowl would be Phoenix, a warm-weather resort community that had already hosted a Super Bowl, and Dallas, which would have a gigantic new stadium coming online and the support of its big-market influential owner, Jerry Jones.

Knowing what we were up against early on—even before we had announced our pursuit of the Super Bowl or organized the bid committee, Bart and I decided that we would do two things that no other Super Bowl bidder had ever done before: (1) raise *all* the money we believed we would need to support hosting the best Super Bowl ever, approximately $25 million, *before* it was awarded to us; and (2) have a bid with *no* public subsidy other than the routine in-kind services from public safety and related agencies. The first commitment would serve at least a couple of purposes. First, successfully doing so should allay any concerns among NFL owners that as a small market, we wouldn't be able to raise the necessary funds to put on a great Super Bowl, and secondly, that it's a helluva lot easier to raise money when you are chasing something rather than after you've caught it. The second commitment, for an unprecedented government subsidy–free Super Bowl, would help generate important public support for the effort.

When I was faxed, right before walking into the hotel conference room in Nashville to make Indianapolis's Super Bowl presentation, the $50,000 pledge that put us over our $25 million goal, we had done what no other prospective Super Bowl host city has ever been able to do: secure all the financial support it needed to raise, and a record amount at that, *before* it was awarded the game. To this day, I am so proud of Indianapolis and the more than one hundred private businesses and individuals who pledged $25 million to support a best-in-class Super Bowl—the largest financial commitment in the game's history. We created a new model on how to fund a Super Bowl.

\* \* \*

Bart and I knew from the beginning that if we were going to be successful, this would need to be a team effort, especially with government and business leaders. This is where Indianapolis has always shone, and we recruited a great team! On January 31, 2007, after seven months of research and groundwork, we announced the launch of Indianapolis 2011 Inc. to secure the Super Bowl, cochaired by Mayor Peterson, Governor Daniels, Colts owner Jim Irsay, and Tony George (then president of the Indianapolis Motor Speedway). I served as president, and our other officers were Cathy Langham (president of Langham Transportation Services), John Lechleiter (then president of Eli Lilly & Company), and Dr. Eugene White (then superintendent of the Indianapolis Public Schools). These were all heavy hitters, but each was personally and actively engaged in the effort. Governor Daniels was incredibly supportive, particularly in helping to secure the state commitments necessary for our bid. Although we had our differences over the stadium/convention center legislation, Governor Daniels could not have been a better teammate throughout the entire Super Bowl effort.

Jim Irsay started our fundraising with an unprecedented $1 million pledge from the host owner, aggressively lobbied his fellow owners, and contributed to the bid lucrative game assets that host owners normally retain for themselves. Tony George brought credibility and insight as the host of the largest single sporting event in the world, the Indianapolis 500. Dr. White brought immense support from the community and helped craft impactful, enduring legacy projects, as described below, critical to our bid. And finally, John Lechleiter and Cathy Langham, as cochairs of the committee's business advisory council, took the laboring oars with me in raising the $25 million in pledges. John Lechleiter's response to our request that he be a key part of our team was typical of that of our other leaders, donors, and volunteers. Bart and I met with John in the bar of the Conrad Hotel, and Bart said, "John, I'm sure you are probably too busy, but we'd like for you to be a big part of this."

Without missing a beat, John said, "I am too busy, but I have to do this because it's too important for our city." I cannot overstate the importance of our team's successful commitment to and hard work on this project, particularly in light of the incredible demands of their real jobs.

I had no idea what an all-in, all-consuming role this would be. Organizing our team, working with the NFL, preparing our bid and presentation, developing political and public support, planning logistics, dealing with the seemingly insatiable media interest, and, most significantly, raising money. I met with Roger Penske—arranged by my friend, then local car dealer Bill Estes—during the 2006 Indianapolis 500 race week to solicit his advice as the leader of the 2006 Detroit Super Bowl effort. Through his good offices, we traveled to Detroit to meet with the other key people involved with Detroit's bid and game. We attended the 2007 Miami Super Bowl and most of its auxiliary events to learn more about putting on the game. We hired PricewaterhouseCoopers to do an independent economic impact study that found that an Indianapolis Super Bowl would bring ninety-eight thousand visitors and $262 million in economic benefit to the Indianapolis region, as well as generate $12 million in net total additional state and local tax revenue. We repeatedly traveled to New York to meet with Commissioner Roger Goodell and former commissioner Paul Tagliabue.

I did basically nothing but work on the Super Bowl effort from that day meeting with the mayor in Dunaway's in early 2006 until we made our presentation to the NFL owners in Nashville on May 23, 2007, well over a year later. I can't say enough about how accommodating and supportive my law partners were, which constituted a large in-kind contribution of my time to the effort by Baker & Daniels in addition to its generous financial one. I was constantly on my phone. One day, I was pulling parent playground supervision duty at St. Thomas and was so engrossed in a Super Bowl phone call that I didn't notice the kickball coming at my head, which literally knocked me down. At my doctor's insistence, I took a little time out to have a regularly scheduled colonoscopy. As they wheeled me in for the procedure, naked under my flimsy robe with back open and untied for obvious reasons, I was on the phone about a Super Bowl issue that couldn't wait. "What are you doing?" the doc who was going to perform the procedure asked me.

"Business," I said.

"You poor dog," said the doc. Until that moment, I didn't even see how ridiculous this was all becoming.

Aware that our competition was stiff and that the owners would have questions about a bid from a northern, small-market city, we threw ourselves into developing a detailed, creative, differentiating bid utilizing the volunteer support of local hospitality industry professionals, event planners, architects, engineers, media experts, educators, and others.

Our bid focused on our strengths. We emphasized who we were and didn't try to be something else. The title of our bid was "Bringing America's Game to America's Heartland" and, among other things, highlighted the following:

- that we were ready as a city developed, built, and operated to be a mecca for major sports events
- that we would have the most convenient and accessible Super Bowl in history with the vast majority of our sports, cultural, and entertainment venues located within the downtown square mile
- our central location, with one-fourth of the NFL's franchises located within four hundred miles of us
- our new state-of-the-art "weatherproof" stadium
- convenient, eclectic, and numerous downtown special-event venues
- a single, unified city-county government in which there was no worry about "navigating the political thicket of competing municipalities" (implicitly drawing a distinction to the Dallas / North Texas bid)
- importantly, enduring legacy projects for the community, including a new first-class, enclosed multipurpose athletic center and the installation of field turf for a new home football field for the Indianapolis Public Schools, as well as establishing the National Youth Fitness Institute to fight childhood obesity

A central feature of our proposal was creating a Super Bowl Village downtown with streetscapes, signage, kiosks, volunteers, building decorations, and special-event programming combined to create a festival atmosphere that would convert Indianapolis's already spectacular downtown into the world's largest party for the NFL, its fans, as well as the Indianapolis citizenry. Perhaps more than anything else, we felt that this "Olympic Village" in the downtown mile square adjacent to the stadium and all the major entertainment venues and hotels would distinguish our bid and our game. It certainly ultimately did so. Of course, a major focus of our bid was that we would have privately raised, before even being awarded the game, a record-setting $25 million to fund our ambitious plans.

We hand-delivered our bid to the NFL headquarters in New York City in eight three-inch binders on April 2, 2007. In addition, to underscore our event experience and give well-heeled decision makers unique, attention-getting memorabilia that even they couldn't otherwise get, along with our very professional executive summary of our bid, we provided an invitation to each owner to attend one of three upcoming Indianapolis sporting events with a special gift representing each event: the 2010 Men's Final Four represented by an NCAA basketball autographed by Larry Bird; the 2010 Western Open represented by a pin flag from Crooked Stick Golf Course autographed by John Daly, who won the 1991 PGA Championship on that course; and an Indianapolis 500 represented by a racing helmet with their team's logo and autographed by Mario Andretti.

The presentation to the owners was on May 23, 2007, in Nashville, Tennessee. I drove down there with my friends and colleagues Deputy Mayor Keira Amstutz and mayoral Press Secretary Steve Campbell. Thanks to the excellent and innovative work of a variety of local professionals, we had developed an amazing, engaging, high-tech presentation for the owners that brought our bid to life and dramatically accentuated its key features. We even got David Letterman to tape a Top Ten List of why Indianapolis should host the Super Bowl. For the presentation we were allowed just five in-person representatives, only two of whom were allowed to speak. Our delegation was made up of NCAA Executive Vice President Tom Jernstedt (an incredible man who sadly passed away in 2020), Emmis Communications Chief Executive Jeff Smulyan, and then Indianapolis Motor Speedway President Tony George, with me and Indianapolis Colts Head Coach Tony Dungy as the designated speakers. During our private rehearsal before the presentation, it was suggested to me that I say a little something about myself to create some familiarity with the owners before I launched into my introduction of our presentation. Based on that advice, I started my presentation with this: "I have been fortunate in my career to work for a US senator, Indiana governor, Indianapolis mayor and even a president of the United States, but the thrill and honor of my professional life is to appear before you to explain why you should want my hometown to host the most important sporting event in the world." I highlighted a few of the key features of our bid, but hit our unprecedented financial model the hardest:

> We are presenting to you today the largest financial commitment in the history of the Super Bowl. We *have* raised and *will spend* on your game at least $25 million *in cash* to take the Super Bowl experience to a whole new level.

That's right, "have raised." Not "gonna raise" or "targeted to raise" or even "will raise." Now. Already. Here's the letters. $25 million from over one hundred private business and individuals: not one dollar in government grants. This $25 million in cash doesn't even include the public and private in-kind contributions worth *millions* of dollars more. That's the kind of commitment *my city* has for the Super Bowl and the NFL.

Tony was awesome, as you would suspect. He told me that he had never lost to Roger Staubach, who was presenting on behalf of Dallas, and he didn't intend to start now! I felt great about our bid and our presentation, and I thought we were going to win. Still, because I felt we had done everything we could do, I was at peace with whatever the outcome would be. We just had to wait on the voting.

Our delegation waited together in our own meeting room, as did the other delegations. We waited a long time. Finally, Pete Ward of the Colts called me and just said: "It's Dallas." I was surprised and crestfallen. Later, Commissioner Goodell came by to tell us the results, compliment us on our bid and presentation, and encourage us to bid again. There had been four rounds of balloting to get the winner the seventeen votes needed to win. Phoenix fell out first, and then it was us against Dallas. We lost 17–15, a vote that could not have been closer. Multiple owners told me and/or Jim that our bid and presentation had been superior to Dallas's in every way but one. The size of the Dallas stadium meant that the NFL owners would make more than $20 million more hosting a Super Bowl there than in the smaller Lucas Oil Stadium. Under those circumstances, it's actually amazing that we came as close as we did.

After we lost the vote that Nashville morning, Keira, Steve, and I headed to Broadway to drown our sorrows. I resisted the temptation to ask the hotel shoeshine guy to return the twenty-dollar tip that I had given him for luck after my shine that morning. We ended up in Tootsie's Orchid Lounge drinking beers and listening to two of the most talented singer/guitar players I've ever heard. They were later joined by a young woman who sang like Janis Joplin, or at least sounded that way after a few hours of Bud Lights.

* * *

The loss in Nashville was almost as encouraging for 2012 as it was discouraging for 2011. We had lost by the smallest possible of margins to a unique venue worth more than $20 million more to the owners. As I told the *Indianapolis Star*, "I think we were like Superman, but unfortunately Dallas was like kryptonite." With Dallas right where we wanted them for 2012—not in the running—the goodwill we had generated from our 2011 bid and presentation, the support of NFL officials and many owners to bid again, including Jerry Jones himself in a personal letter to me, like most knowledgeable observers in football and the media, we felt as though we were a virtual lock to get the 2012 game. The day after the Nashville vote, Bart publicly acknowledged, as reported in the *Indianapolis Star*, that he was ready to try again. Not long after that, I received a thoughtful handwritten note from 2011 cochair Governor Daniels stating, "You're the coach, but we're ready to try again." In light of this strong support and bright prospects, I immediately shifted gears from the disappointment of 2011 to the pursuit of 2012. Our greatest disappointments can create our greatest opportunities if we don't let them deter us.

I knew we needed to capture and maintain our momentum. Obviously, this was on my mind when I told the following to the *Indianapolis Business Journal* the week after Nashville, quoted in an article titled "Too Close to Quit? City Gained Momentum with Super Bowl Bid; New Try Likely": "Sometimes, the way you leave something is as important as how you go in the door. Indianapolis showed it had class, integrity and went into this with the right interests of the NFL at heart. That came through loud and clear. But goodwill like that has pathetically short shelf life" (May 28, 2007). That's good counsel for a lot of situations. When you go out, go out the right way.

With that in mind, we set about already laying the groundwork for a bid on the 2012 Super Bowl. On May 29, 2007, I sent every owner a note thanking them and observing that "even though the final result was not what we had hoped, I do not believe our effort was in vain. Because of our bid, you and many other national leaders know a lot more about the special spirit and attributes of Indianapolis." On June 6, 2007, I had breakfast with Commissioner Goodell in his office in New York, and we had a very positive conversation about Indianapolis getting the 2012 game. For the next several weeks, I had many other meetings and calls with NFL representatives, hospitality industry representatives, government officials, Colts personnel, and others culminating in another meeting with Commissioner Goodell on September 6, 2007, to again advocate for Indianapolis being awarded the 2012 game. Everything seemed to be on track for that to happen.

Then on November 6, 2007, Bart unexpectedly lost the mayoral election to Super Bowl opponent Greg Ballard. I suspected Ballard might change his politically motivated tune after becoming mayor. As I said in my December 17, 2007, letter resigning as president of the Super Bowl bid committee, "In the event the mayor-elect chooses to pursue another Super Bowl bid, I believe he should be able to choose his own person to lead that effort." For me, my resignation from the Super Bowl effort, like that from the CIB, was just the right thing to do. Mayor Ballard did in fact change his tune on pursing the Super Bowl, in record time, by the way, and Indianapolis was ultimately successful in securing the 2012 game on May 20, 2008.

It was very meaningful to me that Bart and I, as noted by the *Indianapolis Star*, were the first two people Jim Irsay thanked that day at the postselection press conference. It was gratifying that a number of other media, political, and sports observers also recognized the contributions that Bart and I had made to Indianapolis being awarded the Super Bowl. Fairly typical of these observations was by the late, great *Indianapolis Star* columnist Matt Tully, who injected this in his column the day after the NFL awarded Indianapolis the Super Bowl:

> Let me stop here for a brief detour. As long as we're talking about the important players in Tuesday's win, it would be negligent not to mention the two most important: Peterson and his long-time adviser on stadium issues, Indianapolis attorney Fred Glass.
>
> Because of the stellar work Glass and his team did last year in bidding for the 2011 Super Bowl, not to mention Peterson's politically risky push for a new stadium in 2004 and 2005, this year's win was essentially guaranteed. So if you're excited about the Super Bowl coming to Indianapolis—and if you're not, check your pulse—thank Peterson and Glass. (May 21, 2008)

I'm proud of the role I had the opportunity to play in Indianapolis very successfully hosting the 2012 Super Bowl. It has been recognized as one of the best ever, fueled by unseasonable sixty-degree-plus weather (much nicer than it was in 2011) and the compact "Olympic Village" celebration atmosphere we were able to create, a central feature of the 2011 bid. I have to agree with the headline of a February 6, 2012, *Forbes* article: "Super Bowl XLVI's Real Winner ? Indianapolis!" which extols how the city's many virtues were highlighted to important corporate decision makers attending the festivities, as well as the many viewers and listeners of impressed media: "Sunday's Super Bowl was the most watched event in American history; the real beneficiary of all that airtime and all those viewers was the city of Indianapolis." Our greatest disappointments can create our greatest opportunities if we don't let them deter us.

# 13. RETURNING TO INDIANA UNIVERSITY

When I heard that Rick Greenspan had resigned as the athletic director at Indiana University in the wake of the Kelvin Sampson NCAA major infractions case, I didn't give it another thought. I had never aspired to that position. It certainly had never been a dream job. I was happy practicing law. Still, after discussing it later with the chair of the search committee, IU Vice President Bill Stephan, I was intrigued, even though if I got the job it would probably mean a couple of hundred thousand dollars a year pay cut. I was forty-nine years old and had been at Baker & Daniels for fifteen years. I had recently read that a midlife career change could be reinvigorating. While I had always, happily, been a "staff guy" in politics, in government, and as a lawyer, I thought it might be fun to run something myself. And not just any something, but an athletic department. At my alma mater. In the quintessential college town of Bloomington, Indiana. On the most beautiful college campus in the country. With college kids. Playing sports.

I had been an IU sports fan for as long as I could remember. In art class in kindergarten, I made the interlocking IU in red and white yarn in an egg carton frame; I had listened to basketball games on a transistor radio through the Lou Watson days; my first football game was with Jimmy Muehler's family (his dad had invented Crest for IU) the year after the Rose Bowl, where we had slid down the grass hills of Memorial Stadium on flattened-out boxes; and my buddy Brian Brase and I skipped school from Brebeuf to welcome the 1976 undefeated national championship team back at the Indianapolis Airport. I was starting to get excited about it. I really wasn't put off too much that I had no experience or expertise in what I was about to take on. I had been to that rodeo before. If IU President Michael McRobbie ended up thinking I could do the job, I'd take it. Accept opportunities presented to you even if you're not sure you are ready, or even capable, because all that matters is that the person offering you the opportunity obviously believes you are.

His wanting me to take it, however, was apparently going to be a bit of a problem. I found out that President McRobbie in his charge to the search committee had said that his single requirement for a successful candidate be that he or she had been an athletic director before because "we have to get someone in here who knows what they are doing!" So I was swimming upstream, to say the least. I did have some things in my favor. Bill Stephan was a law school classmate, and just a few years before, we had worked together when I was Mayor-elect Peterson's transition chair and Bill was outgoing Mayor Goldsmith's chief of staff. Under challenging, highly politicized circumstances, Bill and I had worked together professionally and civilly to do what was right for the city. This is another good lesson in the power of karma. If I had been a jerk, flexing our newfound political muscle in Indianapolis, Bill may well have understandably concluded that I didn't have the temperament to be AD. Bill, I think, was for me, as was his colleague IU Vice President Michael Sample, who, although not on the committee, was an influential advisor to President McRobbie. Mike is a prominent Republican in Indiana, and his experience in public service gave him the belief that my experience in public service would serve me well as AD. My reputation as a bridge builder, not burner, in politics, I suspect, helped me with a senior IU administrative team and "kitchen cabinet" made up primarily of Republicans, other than President McRobbie himself.

I later found out that a well-respected and influential member of the search committee, Jeffersonville businessman Ned Pfau, had been a big advocate for me. I again attributed this to positive political karma, as I had treated Ned with respect as a Republican appointee to the Indiana Port Commission when that body was part of my portfolio as Democratic Governor Evan Bayh's executive assistant for transportation. While his support was political karma, it wasn't the kind I thought it was. The real source of Ned's support was his sister, Barbara House, who along with her husband, John, were Democratic political friends of Evan and, by extension, me. I'd rather be lucky than good.

My most significant ally, by far, was Steve Ferguson, who chaired the board of trustees. Steve was very close to both Senator Bayhs, and Evan was very influential in convincing Steve that I would do a good job as AD. Steve, in turn, I believe, was very influential in convincing Michael that I would do a good job. Especially at the time, I was a highly unconventional choice. Michael was a very new president. For essentially his boss, Steve, to have his back on this decision I'm sure made it an easier one for Michael to make. It all goes back to that internship. I describe these supporters in some detail to underscore my view that there is nothing wrong with calling upon your network to help secure opportunities. In fact, I think it can be an important aspect of making your own luck. Some consider doing so to be somehow mercenary, but I disagree. Although your relationships in life can be happenstance, like Bill Stephan being a law school classmate, or more "earned," like the people I met because I pushed myself out of my comfort zone to take the Birch Bayh internship, they all come back to the person you are. That is, your network is only as good as your earned reputation for being effective, honest, respectful, and the like. When all is said and done, you will have to perform and do the job. Don't be shy about cultivating and utilizing a network. Treat people right. What goes around comes around.

Thus, while my allies were important to my candidacy, ultimately it was up to me to convince the search committee and the president that I was the right person for the job. Once I concluded that this was something I wanted to do, I threw myself into the effort. I read everything I could get my hands on about IU Athletics and intercollegiate athletics in general. I prepared like crazy for my interview with the committee, including for the inevitable question about my total lack of experience for the job. The big day for the interview came. I met with the twenty or so very prominent members of the committee at the Pacers conference room in Conseco Fieldhouse, where committee member Jim Morris was president.

After a fairly long, and I thought positive, interview, the chair thanked me for coming and started to show me the door, but they hadn't asked "the" question. Maybe I had been so brilliant that they weren't concerned about my lack of experience anymore. More likely, they had concluded that my lack of experience was disqualifying, and they were being too polite to bring it up.

After asking if I could make a final comment, I said to the committee, "I appreciate very much the conversation we just had, but during it, I didn't 'Put the Moose on the Table' to quote the title of Randy Tobias's book, which is that I have no experience directly relevant to this job. With your permission I'd like to explain to you why I believe I'm actually the 'low-risk/high-reward' candidate." I think they were a little startled by that, but they told me to go on. I told them why I believed my commitment to, and reputation for, personal integrity would help me reestablish that in an athletic department that had lost it. I told them that my risk management skill set as a lawyer would help me get and keep the department out of trouble. I told them my experience in public service would help me create a transparent culture in the department of which the university could be proud. I told them I had a plan to rebuild the department, including not only the men's basketball program but also, critically, the football program. I told them that I was an Indiana lifer. That I wasn't here to polish things up in the short term so I could get a "better" AD job somewhere else. That I was highly motivated to do things right because I wasn't going anywhere. I would live with the consequences of my decisions even after I was AD because I'd always live in Central Indiana. After that, I think the committee was for me.

I'm told the president's chief of staff telephoned a colleague and said, "Fred Glass just blew up the room," in a good way, I think. Now it was about convincing the president, who went into this thinking he should only hire an experienced AD.

This is where I think Stephan, Sample, and especially Ferguson really came in. President McRobbie trusted them and their judgment, and they all trusted me. Importantly, I think, each of them had been active in government and politics. Steve served in the Indiana General Assembly. They understood how those skills could translate to being the athletic director at a major public research university, which, I believe, properly done, is public service. I met with Steve and President McRobbie at his home in a continuing, amazingly successful effort to keep my candidacy from becoming public. Michael is an intimidating presence. He is a big man with a barrel chest honed from his passion for weight lifting. He is crazy smart. First, he is an academic, and his academic specialty is information technology. Smart on smart! To top it off, his Australian accent adds to the mystique. I had never met him before. We talked for a while, and I made my case similar to how I had with the search committee. Then he asked me if I had any questions, and I said I just had two.

My first question was whether he would commit to me that I would run the department as opposed to power coaches, donors, trustees, or other—even well-intentioned—kibitzers. I told him it wasn't a matter of ego, but if I was going to be accountable, I had to be responsible. His response was something like, "Oh my God, yes!" The first year of his presidency, much to his annoyance, had been consumed with the major infractions case and essentially running the department himself, and he couldn't wait to hand it off lock, stock, and barrel to someone he trusted.

My second question was whether his commitment to excellence that he had shown for teaching, research, rebuilding IU's infrastructure, reestablishing IU's international presence, and the like extended to athletics. I told him I had a good situation in Indianapolis, and I wasn't going to give it up to come down here just to keep the pots from boiling over; rather, I wanted to build an excellent IU Athletic Department. His response was, "I'm an Australian swimmer and cricket player. I'm very competitive. I'm committed to excellence in athletics, and I'll help you get it there." On the drive home, he called me and offered me the job, and I accepted. He said, "Don't accept yet; we haven't agreed on a salary!" Ever the cagey poker player, I told him it really didn't matter. Choose what you judge to be better opportunities over higher salaries.

I note that President McRobbie's steadfast support and leadership were indispensable to what we were able to accomplish at IU Athletics. He never wavered on the commitment to excellence he had given me the day I interviewed with him for the AD job. I appreciated his outstanding leadership and enjoyed what grew to be a trusting friendship.

* * *

I was announced as the new athletic director on October 28, 2008, and people were shocked. Hardly any of my friends knew. It was so out of left field that an old friend of mine, Laura Hughes, called me to tell me that some guy with the same name as me had just been named IU AD! I wasn't starting until January 1, 2009, and Baker & Daniels was very kind to let me use most of my remaining time there to prepare for my new job. I identified about 150 people to interview to start climbing the learning curve and understanding better what I had gotten myself into. I met with university officials, coaches, donors, NCAA regulators, and Big Ten staff, among others. During this process, multiple sitting IU head coaches asked me some variation of the question, "Why would someone who looks like he could be doing something else want to come here to do this?" These questions didn't scare me or make me regret my decision, but they did puzzle and disappoint me. I loved this place so much. The beautiful campus. The quintessential college town. A leading public research university. Kids. Sports. What wasn't to love? But then I tried some Ignation reflection. They clearly felt this way. Why? What was their reality?

Their most significant reality was that I would be the fifth IU athletic director in eight years! Especially looking back, I can't imagine how an athletic department, or any organization for that matter, functions when it is churning leadership like that. Beyond that, the department was barely eight years removed from the firing of legendary IU basketball coach Bob Knight, which had divided not only the department, but the state of Indiana and all of Hoosier Nation; just over a year removed from the tragic death from brain cancer of charismatic IU football coach Terry Hoeppner, who many believed was finally leading IU football out of its perpetual mediocrity; and, the reason the AD job was open, in the midst of a major NCAA rules infractions scandal brought on by our recently fired basketball coach, where we were cheating and apparently not particularly caring about academics, each of which was antithetical to everything that Indiana University liked to believe about itself. All of this had, over time, rocked the department and created morale and dysfunction issues that its members didn't even seem to realize it had because they were their normal.

I quickly came to understand that these circumstances created the kind of issues you might expect with the people in the department. For one thing, they seemed shell-shocked, responding with trepidation—almost fear—over almost every challenge. In my first couple of weeks on the job, the senior staff summoned me to a meeting to tell me about something they thought was a full-blown crisis. After listening without comment to their fairly hysterical presentation, I told them, "Guys, this isn't even in the top two hundred messes I've had to deal with. Let's just relax." A great benefit of having dealt with a number of very challenging, and very public, issues in my previous lives—especially the governor's office at a relatively young age—is that it has given me great perspective on all that has come next.

The staff didn't believe I was coming to stay. There was a widespread rumor—emanating, I believe, from holdover staff who were trying to undercut my ability to make change—that I had taken the job just to raise my profile for a run for governor. People tended just to want to keep their heads down, not get noticed, and endure me as they had endured my predecessors as they quickly passed through. I had experienced a similar phenomenon in government. When we'd win an election, especially like the Indiana governor and Indianapolis mayor races where we were changing parties after decades of control by the other party, we would control the office but not the government, which continued to be controlled by the "we-bes." "We be" here before you got here, "we be" here now, and "we be" here long after your ass is gone! I found that people were afraid to help each other out of fear of also being blamed if something went wrong. They didn't want to take any chances or color outside the lines for fear of being noticed or criticized or failing. I had the sense that the department was just hanging on, trying to make it day-to-day without a real focus on or commitment to creating an excellent experience for our students.

As an example, early in my tenure, I toured the "training table," essentially the cafeteria where our students ate their meals. I noticed that there were two different tables. One had steaks, broccoli, baked potatoes, and fresh salad. The other had chicken nuggets, pizza (which looked to have been of the frozen variety), and applesauce. I asked my senior staff person with me (who oversaw the training table, among other matters) what the deal was with these tables. He told me the first was our "premium" table and the second was the "regular" table. I asked him what the difference was, and he told me that the premium table was for student-athletes who played football and the regular table was for student-athletes who played everything else. I told him, "I'm not going to be the athletic director at a place where a select few eat high off the hog while everyone else watches them while eating crap."

He responded, I swear, "No problem. I'll get some pipe and drape, and we'll separate the premium table students from the regular table students so they don't see each other." That was a huge insight into the mentality of the department. What we did instead was dramatically improve the overall quality of the food that was served to everyone, regardless of their team, and eventually build what became the Tobias Nutrition Center, a roomy, beautiful, state-of-the-art dining hall for our students with floor-to-ceiling windows overlooking the football field, much like a premium club experience in an NFL stadium.

Early in my tenure, I had this Vince Lombardi quote painted on a bulkhead in my office: "Perfection is not attainable, but if we chase perfection, we can catch excellence." This is a reminder to me and my staff that we need to take ownership of every project and take pride in trying to make it perfect. It was born out of a belief that when I first got to IU, too many of our staff had the feeling that "it was good enough for government work"; I was catching sloppy grammar and similar problems with letters and memos right before they were to go out. I made it clear that this was unacceptable, and it quickly became a thing of the past.

The constant changes in leadership and lurching from crisis to crisis were the reality for the coaches asking me why I would take this job and for everyone else in the department. It wasn't normal, but it was their normal. They were dysfunctional with very low morale and seemingly no common purpose, and they didn't seem to grasp that it didn't need to be that way.

I had my work cut out for me.

# 14. HEALING

It quickly became clear to me that before I could really lead the department, I needed to heal it. To do so, I felt we needed to create esprit de corps by rallying around a common sense of who we were, or at least who we wanted to be. For inspiration, I turned to lessons I had learned from the Jesuits. In Jesuit education, particularly at the high school level, there is a concept known as the "grad at grad," which are the characteristics the Jesuits want their graduates to have by the time they graduate. At most Jesuit high schools, like the one I and my four children attended, Brebeuf Jesuit, you can't escape the grad at grad characteristics. Painted on school walls, presented on placards at graduation, and discussed in every class are the five characteristics of the Jesuit graduate at graduation: open to growth, intellectually competent, religious, loving, and committed to doing justice.

So I ripped off the grad at grad. I felt if we articulated a simple set of priorities that we hammered home like the Jesuits as the centerpiece of what the department should be about, we could establish a new, unified, optimistic culture. Even before I officially became AD, I established these four priorities, in order: (1) to play by the rules; (2) to achieve academically; (3) to excel athletically; and (4) to be integrated with the university. The priorities were the foundation of creating a common mission to heal and unite the department.

I came back to Indiana University because of an ugly major infractions case arising from impermissible phone calls and subsequent lying to investigators by then head men's basketball coach Kelvin Sampson. I knew nothing like that could ever be allowed to happen again. The day the NCAA announced its finding on the violations, after I was announced but before I had started as AD, I told the *Indianapolis Star*: "Today the meter starts again on 50 years with no major sanctions." Based on the clearly established "playing by the rules" as our absolute number one priority, we created and maintained a culture of compliance that everyone in the department understood and embraced. We added staff to our compliance office and increasingly hammered home the requirement that everyone follow all the rules. Not just the important ones. Not just the fair ones. Not just the ones our competitors are also following. If you don't think they are the right rules, you need to seek to change them, not ignore them. Importantly, playing by the rules does *not* mean you have to follow the pack, only color inside the lines, accept the conventional wisdom, wait your turn, or—maybe worst of all—do it "because we've always done it this way." No. Those aren't rules; they're excuses.

Especially in light of the Kelvin Sampson debacle, nothing could be more important than complying with all NCAA, conference, and institutional rules. Kelvin Sampson nearly destroyed IU Athletics by breaking a relatively minor rule because he thought it was stupid. That he was probably right about that, given the rule was rescinded a short time after his violation of it, didn't absolve him from his responsibility to follow it. I suggest that if playing by the rules had been the department's number one priority at the time Sampson was being considered for the job, he would not have been hired because he was a documented cheater at Oklahoma.

Priority number two, achieving academically, was also in some ways a vestige of the Sampson experience, and, again, IU should have known better. The graduation rates of the student-athletes in his program at Oklahoma were abysmal. His comment that his "players who wanted to graduate, graduated" should not have been even cold comfort. At Indiana, we were reestablishing that our students participating in intercollegiate athletics were going to go to class and earn Indiana University degrees. This was a value all Hoosiers hold dear and a positive legacy of Coach Knight.

At the same time, we were recommitting to priority number three, excelling athletically. We wanted to be clear that we didn't just want to be "credible" or "competitive," but rather our goal was to win championships. While prioritized behind the threshold values of playing by the rules and graduating, excelling athletically is what an athletic department is supposed to be about, and it is a critical component of our students having a positive experience.

Priority number four, "being integrated with the university," was not only the right thing to do but the smart thing to do. The university is full of great resources that can be used at little or no cost to further the mission of athletics if we are open to them. By embracing the appropriate role of the university administration and the faculty, we could strengthen the initiatives we were wanting to undertake.

Importantly, a couple of years into my tenure, we added a fifth priority. I was challenged by my friend, psychology professor and member of the Bloomington Faculty Council Jim Sherman, to show how the mental wellness of students was addressed in my four priorities. Try as I might, I could not fairly do so. I was resistant to adding any priorities because I stubbornly liked the symmetry of having the same, bedrock priorities since day one. Still, I became convinced that the mental—and physical—wellness of our students was just too critical not to be one of our express priorities. Thus, I added a fifth priority, at priority spot number two in the hierarchy given its relative importance: "being well in mind, body, and spirit." "Mind" and "body" obviously reference mental and physical health. I included "spirit" as a bit of an "empty vessel" for coaches and other staff to help fill with what it might mean for different students, whether spiritual or something else.

The Five Priorities were also the foundation of our creed: "The Spirit of Indiana: 24 Sports, One Team: Impacting Lives, Changing the World," which declares:

> We are able people of integrity who play by the rules.
> We are well in mind, body and spirit.
> We reach our highest academic potential and earn Indiana University degrees.
> We reach our highest athletic potential and win championships.
> We are unselfish leaders and teammates.
> We represent Indiana University with passion, appreciation, respect and distinction.
> We are positive, responsible, inclusive and integrated with our University.
> We are part of something bigger than ourselves.

Like the grad at grad at Brebeuf Jesuit, this "Spirit of Indiana: 24 Sports, One Team" credo was plastered everywhere in the department: framed on the walls of offices, meeting rooms, locker rooms; on the backs of all our business cards; and the like. Every incoming student went through a six-week in-house course teaching the meaning of and purpose behind the Five Priorities and the Spirit of Indiana. We used them as the basis for the annual performance evaluation of every one of our employees. They were the basis on which we hired and fired coaches, made budget decisions, and scheduled our time. For every major decision, I turned to the Five Priorities for guidance, and doing so often made clear the right decision.

What we say about ourselves usually becomes self-fulfilling prophecy even (or especially) if in the short run it is more aspirational than descriptive. The power of this is well captured by the words attributed to ancient Chinese philosopher Lao-Tzu, which I would frequently quote to our staff:

Watch your thoughts;
They become words.
Watch your words;
They become actions.
Watch your actions;
They become habits.
Watch your habits;
They become your character.
Watch your character;
It becomes your destiny.

That is why we have been so mindful with the Five Priorities; the Spirit of Indiana: 24 Sports, One Team; and their progeny to clearly, consistently, and repeatedly declare who we are and who we want to be.

Those words drive who we become.

\* \* \*

Along the way, I discovered that the department was not the only group that needed healing. The most poignant example of this is the IU 10. In fact, it is one of the most meaningful experiences of my entire time as AD, or any other time for that matter.

On February 5, 2015, out of the blue, President McRobbie received a letter from a woman named Trish Geran, who identified herself as "Activist & Author" and "Chairwoman, F Street Coalition." She claimed to represent African American former Indiana University football players, the "IU 10," who had boycotted the 1969 football team over claims of racist behavior by the coaching staff. The letter was unabashedly provocative in tone, making a series of demands, including that the president respond within ten days of the date of the letter or a delay of which "would cause the 'I.U. 10' to demonstrate to outside national mediums, sources, and organizations, which would immediately attach a negative stigma to the school's reputation, something they would rather avoid." She went on to say, "I hope you understand that this is not a cordial form of communication—it is life staking." The president asked me to handle the matter.

My first step, over the understandable objection of some, was to recommend that we meet the ten-day response deadline, notwithstanding that it seemed a bit presumptuous and even unreasonable given that the issues being raised had occurred more than forty-five years before, when none of the current administration was in place. At my request, the president's chief of staff, Karen Adams, responded to Ms. Geran's letter eight days after it was received, advising that we would soon be reaching out to the former player Ms. Geran had identified as the contact person for the IU 10, Michael Adams. Ms. Geran's reply to our response continued to be a little edgy, saying, "This response is very timely. We met Wednesday with the attorney to plan our next move in case you missed the 10 day deadline."

Even though I was only ten years old at the time, I remembered the IU 10. It was the second year after IU had won the Big Ten championship and gone to the Rose Bowl with a young team with a bright future. After shutting out Michigan State on the road 16–0, ten African American players boycotted a practice the next week and refused to return to practice or to play until a series of demands were met involving what they viewed as racist behavior by the coaching staff. Coach John Pont told them if they didn't return to practice, he would kick them off the team; when they didn't, he did. Coach Pont did honor their scholarships, and every member of the IU 10 graduated from Indiana. IU then lost two of its final three games, and the program never recovered, at least under Coach Pont, who left three seasons later for Northwestern. Many felt that the boycott by the IU 10 not only killed the momentum that they had helped create with the 1968 Rose Bowl trip but also contributed to a sense among potential African American recruits that Indiana University wasn't a welcoming place for them. This continued at least until the early years of Pont's successor, Lee Corso, who was known for being supportive of, and close to, his African American players.

It was against this backdrop that we needed to decide what to do next with regard to Ms. Geran's demands. A temptation articulated by some, based on her approach and unclear role with the former players, was simply to ignore or string her out and hope she went away. But it is often more important to pay attention to the message than the messenger. This felt to me like something that would not go away, and perhaps shouldn't go away, as it raised diversity and inclusivity issues about which an organization that claims to hold those as bedrock values ought to care. Moreover, the Jesuit principle of presupposition called us to assume that Ms. Geran and Mr. Adams were coming to us in good faith. Later developments demonstrated they very much were.

I had Mark Deal of our staff call Mr. Adams. Mark's older brother Mike had been on this team. Mark knew Michael Adams and the rest of the IU 10. They, and all the players who played with his brother, had been his heroes. That call went well. We concluded that we should bring the entire IU 10, and Ms. Geran, to campus to talk this through in person. It's so easy to demonize and be suspicious of people you don't know. We further concluded that it would be a hollow invitation if we didn't pay for their travel and lodging, so we did. I drafted a letter to Michael Adams for Karen Adams's signature inviting them to campus, which stated, in pertinent part, the following: "As I am sure you can tell from your conversations with Mark, we are earnestly interested in hearing and better understanding your concerns and those of your teammates whom you have identified. . . . Indiana University considers you, and all of our former students, as family. When families are hurting, they come together, talk, and look for solutions together. That is what we are proposing as the next step here." Always do the right thing, even when no one knows you are or even when the right thing looks to some like the wrong thing.

We set aside a four-day visit, April 7–10, 2015. The university was represented by me; Mark Deal; Vice President for Diversity, Equity, and Multicultural Affairs James Wimbush; Associate Vice Provost and Faculty Athletics Representative Kurt Zorn; Alumni Association Director of Diversity Programs Clarence Boone Jr.; Associate Athletic Director and College Football Hall-of-Famer Anthony Thompson; and Associate Athletic Director/Senior Woman Administrator Mattie White. Five of the eight surviving members of the IU 10 were able to attend: Michael Adams, Charlie Murphy, Benjamin Norman, Clarence Price, and Don Silas, along with Trish Geran.

I thought it was very important to try to build a sense of rapport before we started what I anticipated would be very difficult conversations. Therefore, when they got in on the evening of Tuesday, April 7, we started with a very nice dinner with our guests and the university representatives in the beautiful State Room of the Indiana Memorial Union. We had delightful dinner conversation and talked no "business." I sat next to Trish, and at one point, she asked me if we were going to discuss the matter at hand. I told her that there would be plenty of time for that starting tomorrow; tonight was just for getting to know each other. She seemed surprisingly fine with that. Looking back, I think that dinner was one of the most critical components of the whole process. We needed to see the IU 10 as men, not some characterization in our minds of who they were forty-five years before, and they needed to see us as individuals, not nameless, faceless administrators like those they had pushed up against in their youth.

The next two days were among the most moving and poignant days of my professional life. We met several times, often over meals, and each of the IU 10 shared their very personal and emotional stories of the boycott, what led to it, and its aftermath. Representatives of the university shared as well, particularly those who had endured similar experiences as African Americans. I shared some of what I had been taught about racial justice from the examples of my parents. We cried. We talked. We listened. We hugged. We connected. It was powerful and far exceeded my most optimistic expectations for mutual understanding and, ultimately, reconciliation. Trish Geran, who as you could tell I had my doubts about at the beginning, was a star! She was completely engaged and constantly looking for common ground. These were people I had just met on Tuesday night, and as a result of our intimate and vulnerable sharing, I felt closer to them just by Thursday evening than many people I have known my whole life.

On Thursday evening, based on our conversations, we proposed a series of actions that Indiana University would undertake for the IU 10 as the first concrete steps in an ongoing reconciliation. These included immediate reinstatement to the 1969 football team (including all letterman's club awards and Rose Bowl rings); establishment of a university class for credit that discusses the events leading up to the boycott in 1969 and how conflict resolution may teach us to learn from that; creation of permanent displays in the Henke Hall of Champions and the Neal-Marshall Black Culture Center celebrating the African American student-athlete experience at IU and recognizing the contributions of the IU 10 among others; the taking of their oral history to become a permanent part of the university's archives through the 2020 Bicentennial Project; and their becoming life members of the IU Alumni Association.

Our new friends quickly and graciously accepted our proposal. At their request, we also agreed to make a public announcement sharing the reconciliation of the last three days and arrange a meeting for the IU 10 with President McRobbie in his office. We had an amazing meeting with him there with our entire group, plus Head Football Coach Kevin Wilson and Head Basketball Coach Tom Crean. The comments by the members of the IU 10 were moving and gratifying. Don Silas said, "I'm so pleased that the university was willing to listen to us now in a way I felt they wouldn't in 1969. I feel like the cloud has lifted."

Perhaps my favorite comment came from Charlie Murphy, who succinctly observed, "Our meetings in Bloomington enabled me to leave my bitterness at the Indianapolis Airport on my way back home."

Mike Deal's comments were representative of the reaction of their White teammates: "This is great! We always considered this group to be our 1969 teammates, and we always wanted them to officially be back." I know Mike was proud of his brother Mark's role in the reconciliation. Without Mark's earnest respect for and connection with the IU 10, it simply would not have happened.

In October 2015, we had all living members of the IU 10 and their families back to Bloomington for a special recognition, including at halftime of our football game against Rutgers as well as a part of ceremonies unveiling the IU 10 displays at the Neal-Marshall Black Culture Center and the Henke Hall of Champions. It was a magical weekend to see the pride in those men and by their families in them. Mark kindly shared with me a note Charlie Murphy sent him after that weekend that generously said, in part: "Fred Glass should be very proud of his leadership of cleaning up the past mistakes of those who maybe were not knowing the harm they were causing. When someone can reach back and help that is the mark of leadership."

I'm not going to lie. That means a great deal to me. As I was quoted following the IU 10 meeting with President McRobbie, "The sharing, listening, and understanding that occurred over the three days was nothing less than extraordinary and is one of the great experiences of my professional life. While the process is not complete, the reconciliations we were able to achieve is a testament to what can be accomplished when people of good will come together in good faith to address even the most sensitive and complicated issues." That is the great lesson of the IU 10.

* * *

In any transition, it's good to look for low-hanging fruit to provide early evidence that there is a new and effective approach of leadership, a new sheriff in town, as it were. My early interviews provided just such an opportunity. Many of those I talked to complained about my predecessor being inaccessible. They felt he played favorites with a very small group of coaches and staffers and that if you weren't "in the club," you just didn't matter. As symbolic evidence of this, they often pointed to a locked door that separated the athletic director's suite of offices from the rest of the department. No one could access the athletic director without calling into his assistant and being granted entrance by the door being unlocked from the inside. My first official day, even though it was the New Year's Day holiday, I called Chuck Crabb, who, among other things, oversees our maintenance staff, and told him to take that door down—right off of its hinges. I'm told doing so had its desired effect of being an immediate, very high-profile demonstration that the new leader was going to do things differently, starting with being open and accessible.

There are at least as many definitions of leadership as there are leaders. Here's mine: "Setting and executing a vision with the engagement and support of those you intend to lead." Easy to state and difficult to accomplish. It is the leader's responsibility to identify, articulate, and ultimately accomplish what needs to be done, but not alone. Unless the leader is also able to secure the engagement and support of those he or she intends to lead, he or she will not be successful, or any success will be fragile and short-lived.

As a leader, you have to keep your eyes on the ultimate goal, even when all hell is breaking loose around you. While of course you have to immediately deal with emergencies and take on the alligator closest to the boat, as they say in the navy, over time, you cannot let the urgent displace the important. You must have clearly articulated and understood priorities; if you don't, everyone else's priorities become your priorities. The emails in your inbox, the external requests, the internal meetings, the crisis of the day, and the like can distract you from getting done what you want to get done. I tried to combat that at IU by having a specific "Things to Do" list every week to help me remember what *I* wanted to get done even as I spent, appropriately, considerable time dealing with the unexpected urgent (but not always important!) matters that in the short run demanded my attention. I also made a short (four to five items max) "Things to Do" list for each semester (and the summer) to help me keep my focus on the big things that I wanted to get done to help me avoid getting pulled down by the minutia and waking up at the end of the year with none of the big things accomplished.

It's hard, but critical, to try to identify those big things early. My time in government taught me that administrations, even two terms, move fast and the opportunity to accomplish important things moves fast with them. If you are not thinking at the beginning of your tenure about the big things you want to have accomplished by the end of your tenure, with all the inherent distractions of leading and gestation periods of major undertakings, you may run out of time to get them done. I felt this applied to my tenure as AD, so early on I set the broadly defined goal to rebuild the foundation of IU Athletics, culturally and physically. The details of that I knew would reveal themselves and be developed over time, but from the beginning I was focused on these two things: (1) healing the department and rebuilding a student-centered culture; and (2) rebuilding the department's outdated infrastructure.

We aspired to be the leader in intercollegiate athletics for the care and development of our students. Two of the biggest examples of that were the Excellence Academy and the Student-Athlete Bill of Rights, discussed in chapter 15, but we also pursued a variety of other initiatives. The Drake Group, a national faculty-based organization whose mission is to pursue educational integrity in college sports, recognized through a September 24, 2019, press release that "in April of 2017, the Indiana University athletic department announced what may have been the first comprehensive policy on athlete violence." The Drake Group president, Dr. B. David Ripath, went on to applaud IU Athletics for our "adoption of strong policies sending clear messages to current and prospective athletes that athletics will do their parts to ensure safe college educational environments." I established the Spirit of Indiana Showcase, an annual awards gala celebrating our students' top athletic and academic achievements as well as other talents. At the showcase, I present the Spirit of Indiana Director's Award to the senior male and female students who, on the whole, best personify the tenets of the Spirit of Indiana: 24 Sports, One Team. It was very moving to me when the department, at the last Spirit of Indiana Showcase under my tenure, renamed this award "The G. Frederick Glass Spirit of Indiana Director's Award."

A sign on the door of my office said, "The Director of Athletics can always be interrupted for a Student-Athlete." For one thing, my favorite part of the job is getting to know our students. It also models accessibility, which I think is critical not just for students, but coaches and other staff. We believe that accessibility, that "family feel," is not only the right thing to do, but it is a competitive advantage encouraging collaboration and loyalty.

I also loved getting to know and support our students, as well as the coaches and staff by traveling with the teams to away games. Doing so also served as an opportunity to see the facilities and operations of other Big Ten schools. The dynamic athletic director at the University of Texas, Chris Del Conte, called these trips his "R & D: Rip-off and Duplicate." For example, early on I traveled with our softball team to the University of Michigan for a doubleheader and saw its beautiful softball facilities. I also rode the bus with the baseball team to a game at the University of Louisville's amazing new stadium. This was a raucous trip, by the way, where I had to go through all the rookie rituals of singing and being quizzed on obscure questions, such as, "If you had to come back as an animal, which one would it be and why?" It reminded me of the bus scenes from the movie *Bull Durham*. These trips really opened my eyes to the need to substantially upgrade our very poor softball and baseball facilities. My most consistent team travel was to virtually every away football game with Barbara. These trips really drove home to me how far behind we were in our football facilities and how much investment it would take to catch up if we wanted to be competitive in football—and we needed to be competitive in football. I also traveled with the teams to many away men's and women's basketball games, including almost every men's game in Tom's first year because I felt that he and the team needed to see my support during that uniquely challenging time.

By honoring our priorities and living our values, I believe we healed the department and were leading it to achieving our ultimate goal of developing our students better academically, athletically, and personally than any other athletic department in the country and by so doing, were establishing a new golden age of Indiana University athletics.

# 15. LEADING AND REBUILDING

One of my heroes and a role model for me as I worked to lead the Athletic Department was Herman B Wells, the eleventh president of Indiana University, who served as such from 1938 to 1962. I had a large framed picture of him in my office to remind me of his wisdom and strength. Wells was the transformational leader of Indiana University's illustrious history, moving it from a rather unremarkable, parochial college into a world-class, internationally recognized institution of higher learning. He did so through innovation, but with a great common touch, and with a constant focus on and love for his faculty and students.

An IU alumnus, Wells was appointed dean of IU's School of Business at just thirty-one years of age. When the presidency became open two years later, Wells shrewdly offered to the board to serve as acting president since, he coyly observed, because of his youth he wouldn't be considered a candidate for the permanent job. He proved to be such an adept administrator, and politician, that the board later unanimously elected him president. He was inaugurated as the nation's youngest state university president on December 1, 1938, at the age of thirty-six.

Wells was both an innovative visionary and practical executive. He recruited internationally acclaimed faculty; expanded the campus and student enrollment; built a world-class language program, music school, business school, arts program, and program of international study and engagement; and beautified the campus through building design and greenspace preservation. Wells famously pronounced, "To cut a tree unnecessarily has long been an act of treason against our heritage and the loyalty, love and effort of our predecessors who have preserved it for us." His actions and example have made IU-Bloomington one of the most beautiful college campuses in America. Even in conservative Indiana, Wells was able to be a leader in civil rights and academic freedom through an innate ability to quietly, but effectively, envision and achieve major change without antagonizing political and business leaders who otherwise might have effectively opposed him. Among other things, he was a leader in ending racial segregation practices in Bloomington, on and off campus; led the end of the Big Ten's "gentlemen's agreement" by supporting the recruitment of African American Bill Garrett to play basketball for IU; and championed academic freedom, including his support of IU professor Alfred Kinsey's study of human sexuality.

Although I never knew Wells, two books made me feel as if I had: Wells's autobiography, *Being Lucky: Reminiscences and Reflections*, as well as the biography *Herman B Wells: The Promise of the American University*, by James H. Capshew. Barbara gave me *Being Lucky* on my appointment as athletic director with the inscription, "To Fred, who makes his own good luck. I love you." I used *Being Lucky* as a guide in leading the department as AD from my preappointment transition on. I have taken as his most significant lesson that to have a great organization, you have to have great people and that to attract and retain great people, they have to know they are sincerely valued and an important part of something important bigger than themselves. I have also embraced his admonition to "dream no small dreams for they lack the passion to stir men's blood." He may have gotten a little inspiration on this one from Goethe, but the lesson to think big is a good one. It also sounds a bit like the magis, and Ignatius would certainly approve. We robustly applied it in IU Athletics, such as in investing nearly a third of a billion dollars in just over a decade to rebuild the aging infrastructure of IU Athletics.

\* \* \*

I have long believed that being a value-based organization is a critical component to achieving one's priorities, particularly during this era of unprecedented change in intercollegiate athletics. Although values are fairly easy to recite, they can be hard to live. As my friend Pete Yonkman, CEO of Cook Inc., once told me, "Value-based organizations truly earn their claims to be such in tough times." Dr. Tim Elmore, a best-selling author and international speaker who has presented to the department many times, also recognizes the especially important role values play in tough times. He suggests that during uncertain times, leaders need to utilize a "compass" rather than a "GPS" to find the way. He says, "A GPS or Google Maps will be helpful only if you are on paved roads with names on them. If you are entering new areas, you need a compass that shows you true north. Similarly, we need values that provide direction when we enter new territory."

We articulated the principal values for IU Athletics in the Five Priorities and the Spirit of Indiana: 24 Sports, One Team. Still, there are a number of additional bedrock values that I believe are critical for any organization and were certainly critical for IU Athletics. We constantly communicated and discussed these values in a variety of ways with and among our staff, including me presenting them to the entire three-hundred-plus members of the department at least once a year during my annual all-staff address.

## 1. BE POSITIVE AND HAVE FUN

Optimism and belief are competitive advantages. I learned this long ago from Evan's historic highway commissioner, Chris Letts, who I introduced earlier. Chris and I would be working on really challenging issues, and I'd get very frustrated with the problem and/or the people involved, yet Chris would maintain this sunny disposition. *That* started to frustrate me too, so I asked her about it. She told me rather matter-of-factly that she used to let problems get her mad, but she realized getting mad was counterproductive to solving problems, so she just decided to stay positive and forward-looking and resist being emotional and looking back for someone to blame. She just decided. Positivity, like happiness, is a choice.

Being positive and optimistic is a self-fulfilling prophecy. It makes you a better friend, colleague, and family member. As a small example, if anyone asks how I am or how I'm doing, I *always* say, "Excellent!" Unfortunately, that appears to be unusual enough that I often get strong, surprised reactions from people who are positively taken back by my response. This belief in optimism is also why I had these two quotes printed on the walls of our weight room: "Fortune favors the bold," Homer, and "Excellence is a habit," Aristotle. Especially after you embrace optimism, follow the advice I once heard from a coach: "Always talk to yourself; never listen to yourself. Feed the positive, reduce the negative."

## 2. BE FORGIVING AND GRATEFUL

I've long believed that forgiveness and gratitude are the twin secrets to a happy life. Forgiving others doesn't make you a chump or a doormat. Forgiveness frees the forgiver. And although it is obviously very important for the big things, it is also very important for the little things because that's where we live our lives. A fellow motorist's incivility, curtness from a tired spouse, insensitivity from a coworker, selfishness from a child, and lack of caring from a service provider are just a few examples of opportunities to forgive minor transgressions that can have a powerfully positive impact on your outlook, your attitude, and therefore your life. Similarly, gratitude is clearly important for the big things and, perhaps ironically, I think is easiest for the big things, such as a positive diagnosis, the birth of a child, a promotion at work, and the like. But like forgiveness, and for the same reason, it may be most important for the little or overlooked things, like our health—which gets overlooked less the older we get—the curiosity of a child, the patience of a spouse with one of our shortcomings, and the like. Psychologists tell us we are evolutionarily hardwired to focus on the headwinds as a matter of survival so that we can see and address threats. Unfortunately, if we let it, doing that can crowd out our appreciation for the plentiful tailwinds, the gratitude for which can be empowering and reassuring.

## 3. Be Kind

It seems crazy even to have to say this one, sort of like, "Please don't eat the daisies." Unfortunately, particularly in the current political climate and era of social media, we need to be expressly mindful of being nice. Many politicians, cable TV commentators, and internet trolls are constantly telling us in the most mean-spirited ways to be afraid of each other, don't trust "them," and the like. People are so preoccupied on their phones that we are ironically losing the personal connectivity that binds us together. Foster civility, kindness, and respect in your organizations both by modeling it and demanding it. This should include "honoring the absent," as Father Jim Martin, SJ, calls us to do, which in essence means not to talk behind other people's backs. I've found a simple rule for this is try not to say anything *about* someone you wouldn't say *to* someone.

## 4. Presume Good Faith

As you may recall, the Jesuits refer to this as the Presupposition. It calls on us to come to interactions with others presuming that they are also coming to the interaction in good faith. It's amazing how much you can get done when you assume people want to help you to succeed, especially if they feel you respect and trust them. Now, the Presupposition doesn't mean that in fact everyone has good faith, just that most do and to assume otherwise harms *your* ability to get things done. In an organization that practices the Presupposition, it is easier to identify and deal with those who demonstrate bad faith.

## 5. Be Loyal

Loyalty, and the trust it begets, is critical but potentially dangerous because blind loyalty is not loyalty. The leader must create an environment in which people are willing to appropriately challenge and test the views of the leader. An old political saying applies here: "If the officeholder is dumb, he or she needs to surround himself or herself with smart people; if the officeholder is smart, he or she needs to surround himself or herself with people that disagree with him or her all the time."

## 6. Connect With Each Other

Especially in this age of email and social media, people need to affirmatively resist the convenience and danger of technology and directly interact in person as much as possible. The *e* in email stands for "eternal" and "evil." Electronic communication is susceptible to misinterpretation, never goes away, and can be seen by people not originally privy to the conversation, especially with public universities, government, and almost anyone else through litigation or a regulatory/criminal investigation. Look for opportunities to forgo texts and emails where you can in favor of picking up the phone or, better yet, going to see somebody.

## 7. Take Your Job Seriously, Not Yourself

It's very important that we keep separate our individual personal identities and the official positions we hold at work. Our jobs are what we do, not who we are, and we can't let them define us. Whether in my role as Evan's chief of staff or IU's AD, I always understood that those jobs were bigger than me and I was just their temporary steward.

From early on in my tenure as AD, I looked for ways to show that although I respected my job, I didn't take myself too seriously. This was particularly important with my staff, intimidated by the thought of this politician lawyer who didn't know anything about athletics coming down from Indianapolis. For that reason, I never wore a suit or tie to work, instead always dressing in IU polo shirts and pullovers, including in my official department photograph. I'm told this had the desired effect of helping put people at ease.

## 8. Care for the Whole Person

As we've already seen, the Jesuits call this *cura personalis*, and as noted earlier, it was the inspiration for the IU Athletics Excellence Academy, which, as discussed in more detail below, is committed to the holistic personal development of every one of our students who participate in intercollegiate athletics.

## 9. Promote Diversity and Inclusivity

This is not only the right thing to do, it is the smart thing to do to make sure we are recruiting and retaining the best people and that we are well positioned to interact with customers and others who also value diversity and inclusivity, specifically including race, sexual orientation, religious affiliation, and gender identity. A corresponding component of *cura personalis's* care for the whole person calls us to respect all that makes up every individual, especially differences, and to recognize that individuals with differences from the main community are in a position to contribute particularly valuable perspectives for the rest of the community.

In the fall of 2016, after that very acrimonious presidential campaign that had racist, homophobic, and anti-immigrant overtones, I established the Athletic Director's Council on Diversity and Inclusivity to provide a forum to a representative group of students from all our teams to discuss such issues and how we could maintain and improve IU Athletics as a safe, welcoming place for diverse students. Earlier, we had been one of the first athletic departments in the country to participate in Gay Pride parades and other activities. IU Athletics was one of only eight Power Five athletic departments to earn a perfect LGBTQ Athletic Equality Index score from Athlete Ally. I'm a proud member of the IU LGBTQ+ Alumni Association.

## 10. Follow the Platinum Rule

We all know the Golden Rule. The Platinum Rule puts an important twist on it: "Treat others like *they* want to be treated." This is particularly, but not only, important to help make a diverse organization also inclusive. Perhaps the way I would like to be treated isn't the same as the way you would like to be treated given your background, life experiences, personality, or any number of other reasons. For a relatively recent and random example, when Barbara turned sixty, I didn't throw her a big party with all her friends, even though that's what I would have wanted (and got from her when I turned sixty eleven months later). Because she doesn't like to be the guest of honor at big events, I instead took her on a trip. We were treating each other as we knew the other wanted to be treated, not how we wanted to be treated.

## 11. Be Demanding, but Not Demeaning

This had obvious application to the coaches under my charge, and I reminded them frequently of this expectation. Hall of Fame Buffalo Bills

Coach Marv Levy used to say, "Criticize the play, not the player." While it's easy to focus on the "not demeaning" part, the "be demanding" part is equally important, for it is when coaches push their players outside of their comfort zones to accomplish things they did not think possible that the magic happens and championships are won. This is applicable beyond coaches and players to all leaders and followers.

## 12. We Are What We Tolerate

This admonition reminds us that if leaders allow inappropriate behavior in their organizations, those behaviors become a part of what that organization is and can't be simply dismissed as "Bill being Bill" or "Jane being Jane." This value weighed heavily on me in the separation of Kevin Wilson as our head football coach. The team was performing quite well, but Kevin and I were not on the same page in how it was being led.

## 13. Take Criticism Seriously, Not Personally

As the athletic director at Indiana University, I had ample opportunity to apply this maxim. Leaders must listen to criticism, internal or external, and resist the temptation, especially during challenging times, to "go into the bunker" with your colleagues and allies and ignore it. Consistent with taking your job seriously, not yourself, criticism should be objectively and dispassionately evaluated. I would often tell our staff that criticism is not to be feared because it either has merit or it doesn't. If the criticism has merit and needs to be addressed, it's just given you an opportunity to get better. Don't be defensive; address it. On the other hand, if you conclude the criticism does not have merit and doesn't need to be addressed, then don't worry about it and be happy that it's not a problem. Again, don't be defensive; move on. We defeat criticism by embracing it. In a similar vein, if something negative leaks out of your organization, don't ask, "Who told?" Ask, "Is it true?" Leaders can get so preoccupied with plugging leaks that they don't give appropriate attention to the underlying problem being exposed. My experience is that if you can take care of the underlying problem, the leaks take care of themselves.

## 14. Do the Right Thing

This is the most important and useful value of them all. Eleanor Roosevelt really captured it when she said, "Do what you feel in your heart to be right, for you'll be criticized anyway." In athletics, as with politics and I suppose most other things, no matter what you chose to do, you will be criticized—so you might as well do what you think is right. As long as

I can look myself in the mirror and my family in their eyes and be confident that I did the right thing as best I could determine it, then I'm at peace no matter the criticism or consequence. It's a fool's errand to try to make decisions to avoid criticism, be popular, or look as if you are doing the right thing. Sometimes doing the right thing means doing the thing that looks like the wrong thing, especially when you are privy to facts unknown to others. That eminent philosopher Dr. Seuss understood the importance of doing the right thing when he observed, "Be who you are and say what you feel because those who mind don't matter and those who matter don't mind." I actually think of the Seuss quote often and take great comfort in it. Often you will be faced with a tough decision with each choice having its upsides and downsides. You may be tempted to "split the baby," or somehow blend the choices into a compromise decision. Be very careful with this. Sometimes when you try to get the best of both worlds, you end up with the worst. Pick your poison. Choose the position you would feel most comfortable defending. Always do the right thing, even when no one knows or appreciates that you are and even when the right thing looks like the wrong thing.

\* \* \*

As noted earlier, our ultimate goal for Indiana University Athletics was to develop our students academically, athletically, and personally better than any other athletic department in the country. Our commitment to that goal is most tangibly evidenced by the Circle of Excellence, which we built in Memorial Stadium. Indiana University Athletics is the only athletic department in the country to have located on its campus in one place first-in-class facilities dedicated to the academic, athletic, and personal development of students participating in intercollegiate athletics.

**D. Ames Shuel Academic Center.** The previous "academic center" when I got back to Indiana was a glorified hallway in Assembly Hall that couldn't have been two thousand square feet. Kids would be doing their work sitting on the floor with their aptly named laptop computers. It was awful. To address these issues, in 2011, we spent $3 million to build out the 25,800-square-foot D. Ames Shuel Academic Center on the east side of Memorial Stadium to provide our students with the academic resources they need, including new technology, classrooms, lecture facilities, study areas, spaces for private sessions, and offices for academic advisors. To address turnover resulting from noncompetitive pay, we also dramatically increased the salaries for our academic advisors from funds saved by eliminating several senior management positions.

During my last year as AD, we set a graduation success rate (GSR) record of 91 percent, the eighth straight year IU had either established or tied a GSR record and a dramatic improvement over the 77 percent GSR I essentially inherited in 2011. During my tenure, we also set all-time school records for Academic All-Big Ten honorees, Big Ten Distinguished Scholars, Academic Progress Rate (APR) scores, number of teams with perfect single-year APR scores, and combined grade point average.

**W. Jay and Nancy Wilkinson Performance Center.** One of the largest strength and fitness centers in all of intercollegiate athletics, this twenty-five-thousand-square-foot facility was completed in 2009 as part of an even larger $49 million student-athlete development center closing in the north end zone of Memorial Stadium. It services all our students with the latest in strength and fitness training equipment and technology.

While I was AD, twenty-five teams and 210 individuals won conference championships; 46 students were named Big Ten Player of the Year in their respective sports; 537 students earned All-American honors (including a school record 91 in 2017–2018); 3 were named Big Ten Athlete of the Year (before my arrival, it had been nineteen years since an IU athlete had won the award); 26 coaches were named conference coach of the year; 5 coaches were named national coach of the year; 28 individuals won national championships; and one team won a national championship.

**Excellence Academy.** Early in my tenure as athletic director, we established the Indiana University Excellence Academy Program dedicated to the personal development of our students participating in intercollegiate athletics. I believe the Excellence Academy was and is the most innovative and comprehensive personal development program in all of intercollegiate athletics. Consistent with the Jesuit concept of *cura personalis*, the Excellence Academy focuses on the holistic development of the entire person to develop healthy students with a toolbox of skills and resources to provide an exceptional college experience, including athletics, which will prepare them for an outstanding life experience after athletics. In the fall of 2018, the Excellence Academy program expanded and became housed in a brand-new $48 million, 66,575-square-foot Excellence Academy building enclosing the south end of Memorial Stadium. There is no other program or building in all of intercollegiate athletics so completely and effectively dedicated to the personal development of its students. Barbara and I were pleased to make a six-figure gift to the Excellence Academy to support the

Glass Family Leadership Suite, where student leaders can meet and/or enjoy a quiet study area.

* * *

Part of leading the department back to where we wanted it to be had to include rebuilding its infrastructure. When I returned to Bloomington as the athletic director in 2009, the athletic facilities did not look a whole lot different than when I had left as a graduating senior twenty-eight years earlier in 1981. That we had substantially fallen behind our Big Ten peers in facilities became clearer and clearer the more Big Ten campuses I visited with our teams. During my tenure, we completed a nearly third-of-a-billion-dollar investment to renovate and expand IU's aging facilities, substantially based on aggressive private fundraising and all without the use of any tuition contribution, student fee, or taxpayer money. This initiative greatly enhanced the experiences of our students, as well as their ability to compete for championships, and will continue to do so for generations to come.

Every one of our facility projects has its own interesting story to tell from design, to fundraising and funding, to approval, and to construction. For illustrative purposes, I will describe in a little more detail two of the most important, and intertwined, facility projects we completed: the renovation of Simon Skjodt Assembly Hall and the establishment of the Mark Cuban Center for Media and Technology.

When I became the AD at Indiana, there were already discussions among university leaders about razing Assembly Hall and building a new basketball arena. The chairman of the board of trustees, Steve Ferguson, who had been instrumental in me becoming AD, advocated a new arena. My predecessor had commissioned a study that favored a new arena. The site for what would become Cook Hall had been relocated, at some considerable expense, to accommodate a new basketball arena to the south of Assembly Hall.

I did not favor a new basketball arena. First, Assembly Hall is one of the most iconic venues in all of college basketball. Famed broadcaster Gus Johnson called it "the Carnegie Hall of college basketball." It provides our programs the best home court advantage in college basketball. Survey after survey of coaches and players identified Assembly Hall as the toughest place to play in the Big Ten, which is home to some of the best home court advantages in college basketball. I did not want to replace the best home court advantage in college basketball in one of its most iconic arenas with a cookie-cutter, multipurpose, you-could-be-anywhere building as was done, for example, at Ohio State (replacing St. Johns Arena), Wisconsin (replacing Wisconsin Field House), and Michigan State (replacing Jenson Field House).

Second, the estimated $350 million cost to design and build a new arena, even if we could have raised enough money to support it, would have sucked all the air out of all the many other facility projects we needed to undertake: $350 million would have been more than every capital project we were able to complete in my nearly twelve years at Indiana combined! I believed that we could preserve and improve our iconic venue and home court advantage for not much more than 10 percent of what a new arena would cost, and I set about convincing reluctant decision makers to let me do just that.

Of course, in the end we were successful with this approach, based in part, I believe, in relentlessly describing this project as "preserving the best home court advantage in college basketball," which appealed not only to Hoosier pride but our desire to return to our glory days and maintain every advantage available to do so. Branding the project in this way was reminiscent of how we had successfully branded the "midfield terminal project" as the new Indianapolis Airport.

We initially estimated it would cost around $40 million for the kind of renovation we needed for Assembly Hall, including addressing the boring stuff like outdated mechanical, electrical, and plumbing issues, plus more exciting features like a grand new entryway and plaza facing campus, replacing the ramps with escalators, replacing all the seats, a giant new videoboard, and adding premium viewing areas—all without losing the quintessential Assembly Hall feel. As with our solution from my days in Indianapolis to save the Colts, secure Final Fours, and preserve the hospitality industry through a new stadium and expanded convention center, I felt we needed to make sure the public understood our problem of a run-down Assembly Hall before they would support fixing it. That's why we started a drumbeat about the need to address long-deferred maintenance and otherwise modernize Assembly Hall to preserve the best home court advantage in college basketball before we proposed the renovations. When around that time a large piece of metal fell from the Assembly Hall ceiling into a seating area that only a few hours later would have been filled with fans for our game against Iowa, there was an increased public understanding of the urgency of proceeding with the renovation.

We were hoping for a major gift to cover the entire cost of the project. The question then became who. My first target, perhaps predictably, was IU alumnus Mark Cuban. Mark had famously made his original fortune by creating a company that ultimately became broadcast.com so that he and his IU alumni buddies in Dallas could listen to radio broadcasts of IU games in real time by streaming them on the internet. It was a concept Mark invented.

Mark and I were IU classmates, and although we had friends in common, we didn't know each other at IU. I had, however, spent considerable time as an IU student in the bar he bought, Motley's Pub. After I became AD, I started to reach out to Mark occasionally, especially when he would return to campus for various events. While perhaps already an obvious fundraising target, I got more focused on approaching Mark with a proposal based on some intelligence shared with me by IU alumnus and well-known filmmaker Angelo Pizzo (*Hoosiers; Rudy*), who got to know Mark while filming him in a commercial to promote IU. These commercials always end with the tagline, "If it wasn't for Indiana University, I wouldn't be here." Angelo told me when Mark filmed that line, he playfully added, "At Mark Cuban Assembly Hall." He was just goofing around, but under the theory that there are no truer words than those said in jest, I accelerated thinking about how to approach him for a gift to renovate and name Assembly Hall.

Mark and Anthony Thompson had struck up a friendship when they played basketball together at a Tom Crean fantasy basketball camp. AT, a college football hall-of-famer, was a senior member of my staff and also one of the best football players ever at Indiana. Through his good offices, we flew down to Dallas to meet with Mark in October 2013, and I pitched him on funding the renovation of Assembly Hall. It was no dice from jump street. Mark, a well-known critic of the escalating costs of higher education, believed philanthropically funding university facilities contributed to that escalation by building in increased maintenance and other costs. I tried to point out that wouldn't be the case with athletic facilities because athletics was financially independent from the university and therefore couldn't contribute to increased tuition costs. He was unconvinced. I asked him if there was anything he would consider helping to fund. He told me that he would entertain a proposal, the more innovative the better, to utilize differentiating technology education to develop the kind of graduates that he'd like to hire someday. With that, after a very pleasant meeting, AT and I left.

Although we didn't get a yes on a gift for Assembly Hall, both AT and I knew that the meeting had been successful. We had nurtured a positive relationship with Mark and had gotten a very good feel for where his philanthropic interests might lie. This is an example of a concept that is important in almost any undertaking: Sometimes it is a big win just to live to fight another day. Whether it's soliciting a donor, seeking an administration approval, or trying to get a stadium built, the road is not usually paved with a string of yeses. But avoiding a final and definitive no, to keep the process alive until you can take the next step, can be the best path to success.

We then turned our attention for an Assembly Hall gift to IU alumna and philanthropist Cindy Simon Skjodt, who is the daughter and niece of the mall magnate brothers Mel and Herb Simon, respectively. Cindy had been in Barbara's class at IU, and although they also didn't know each other, they had many common friends. I knew Cindy a little bit from Democratic politics, and she had a good friendship as a result of her longtime financial support of IU Athletics with my deputy athletic director Scott Dolson. Cindy *loves* IU basketball. As we started talking to her about a potential gift, we learned how deep that love ran. It seems that IU basketball games were something she and her dad found time to share even as he was busy growing his very successful business. Going to IU basketball games was one of the main things they were able to share. As a committed philanthropist, and cochair of our just announced Bicentennial Capital Campaign for IU Athletics, Cindy was also committed to helping get the campaign off to a great start and thereby set an example and create momentum for a successful campaign.

Scott Dolson, Tom Crean, and I went to Cindy's beautiful home to meet with her and her husband, Paul, to describe our vision for what a renovated Assembly Hall could be and how her early major lead gift could spur a great deal of additional philanthropy for the campaign. Tom in particular did a great job in demonstrating his support and real passion for the project. Cindy essentially agreed to our $40 million gift request right then and there, but that gift had been in the making since that little eight-year-old girl and her father first walked hand in hand into Assembly Hall. It was the largest gift for a capital project in the history of IU Athletics. I was so pleased that Cindy also agreed to put her name on the building. Simon Skjodt Assembly Hall stands as an inspiration for Hoosiers who grow up loving Indiana basketball and the dramatic impact of philanthropy. It was particularly moving for me to see how our female students, especially on the women's basketball team, reacted when they heard that a woman was responsible for preserving the best home court in college basketball. It helped them believe that they could accomplish anything.

Meanwhile, we hadn't lost track of Mark. Social media graphics, videos, and other electronic communication were starting to overtake the traditional ways we communicated with our fans, donors, recruits, and other constituencies. I found that although our existing staff was great at knocking out a press release, drafting a recruiting letter, or producing a highlight reel for the team awards banquet, a freshman with a laptop sitting in the hallway waiting for a class was way ahead of them in producing the kind of social media content and electronic communication that our fans and recruits really wanted. I wanted to create a way to match up our need for that expertise with the students on campus, who, as natives to this technology rather than immigrants like the rest of us, could meet that need in spades (using grandpa language here underscores my point). We imagined a program where we harnessed on-campus student talent excited to ply their skills at IU Athletics and build a portfolio of their work for future employers to help us be on the cutting-edge of creating this content. In fact, we had tentatively plugged into our capital campaign plan to raise funds for some sort of center for sports media and technology. And that's the next idea we took to Mark, who again had told us he was interested in helping us develop the kind of students he would want to hire someday.

We had considerable internal debate about how best to present the idea to him. My staff ultimately recommended a multiperson super-high-tech presentation with laptops, holograms, interactive displays, and the like. In my due diligence, I had found an October 8, 2014, interview of Mark by Colin Cowherd on his show *The Herd*. Cowherd asked him what turned him off and on by presenters on *Shark Tank*. Mark told him he loved the "big vision" but that he hated "the backstory": "The more you tell me about your troubles, the more you tell me about your background, the less time you have to tell me about the business, and I am out." I wrote just five points on a three-by-five card and in January 2015 flew back down to Dallas with AT to meet again with Mark. He pulled up a little sweaty in workout clothes, and we met in a small conference room at the airport. I barely got out my first few points, telling him that I wanted him to give us a major gift, not to fund a new building, but new technology to produce cutting-edge social media, virtual reality, augmented reality, 3D replay, and ... he put up his hand as if to tell me to be quiet. "I could get behind that," he said. "I'll give you five million dollars to start." Bingo! That was eerily the amount I was going to request! I thanked him and got the hell out of there. I had long ago learned to stop talking as soon as you get the business.

In March 2015, I met Mark in the bar of the Conrad Hotel in Indianapolis when he was in town for his Mavericks to play the Pacers. I wanted to name this program/facility for him, and he had declined. He didn't want to. He thought it too self-aggrandizing. I said to him, "Look, Mark, letting us use your name would be a major part of the gift to *us*! There is no name in America that more personifies sports, media, *and* technology than yours. Please let us use it to attract students *and* technology from the most cutting-edge companies." He reluctantly did. On June 5, 2015, along with President McRobbie, Mark and I announced his $5 million gift and the establishment of the Mark Cuban Center for Media and Technology, during which he said, "Whatever I give to IU, it will only be a fraction of what IU gave to me." How about that? It was so good, I put it on a billboard.

Fittingly, we housed the Cuban Center in the newly renovated Simon Skjodt Assembly Hall. Without question, the center has been a resounding success, putting Indiana University at the forefront of media technology and developing the kind of students Mark Cuban wants to hire and has hired. For example, the live production experience one of our students obtained through the Cuban Center led to her obtaining a senior-level position with the Kennedy Center right out of IU. The company that produces and installs 3D replay technology in sports venues worldwide utilized Cuban Center students to help install it in Simon Skjodt Assembly Hall and Memorial Stadium (the first college in America to utilize such technology in not only one but both of its most significant venues) and *then* turned around and hired several of them, at six-figure salaries, to travel the world installing the technology in other venues.

Perhaps as a vestige of my political campaign and Super Bowl bid days, I confess to having been a shameless fundraiser at IU. We set six all-time annual fundraising records in my last nine years, secured seventeen of the eighteen largest gifts in IU Athletics history, and raised more than triple the funds in gifts of more than $1 million than in the entire rest of the history of IU Athletics. We shattered our goal for the Bicentennial Capital Campaign for IU Athletics by raising $225 million. Of course, the credit for this success belongs to our generous donors, outstanding development staff, and amazing volunteer supporters, particularly those who have served on our Varsity Club National Board of Directors.

* * *

In 2013, I was meeting with a freshman in high school whom we were recruiting for volleyball and her parents. This family was early on the circuit, and I was surprised how little they understood about the benefits of being a student who participates in intercollegiate athletics. Not too long before, a cover story in the *Atlantic*, depicting an African American in shackles, had likened participating in intercollegiate athletics to slavery. While there clearly had been, and in some cases still were, overreaching and abuses of students in intercollegiate athletics that needed to be addressed, I couldn't help but feel that this article and similar criticisms overlooked the positive impact of intercollegiate athletics on our students participating in them.

I set about to identify and list what we were doing and/or should be doing for our students so that we could announce it to the world and thus be held to account for it. I felt this would provide much-needed information to recruits like my high school freshman volleyball player; a counterweight to the emerging conventional wisdom that our students were only being exploited; and tangible commitments that would rightly become expectations for our students and their families. It was a tremendous exercise. I kicked it off by spending my spring break with Barbara, somewhat to her chagrin, by a pool in Florida taking the first stab at what a Student-Athlete Bill of Rights might look like. I suppose it was an occupational hazard as a lawyer and student of politics and history to think about such a project in those terms.

Later, as a staff, we really dug into what we were doing as a department for our students and what we ought to be doing. We constantly evaluated if we should stop doing/requiring certain things detrimental to some or all of our students or, conversely, start doing/requiring certain things beneficial to some or all of our students. A number of times we would realize we were 82 percent on our way to doing a good thing, and we added the final 18 percent so we could actually do it (and get credit for doing it!). We ended up with an unprecedented, innovative vehicle that documented and committed us to a variety of things that we were both already doing for our students as well as new—in some cases—groundbreaking benefits that we—and almost every other school in intercollegiate athletics—had never before offered.

First, we broke down any and all distinctions among revenue, nonrevenue, male, and female athletes and even—other than the amounts of their grant-in-aid—among full-scholarship, partial-scholarship, and walk-on athletes. Thus, *every* student participating in intercollegiate athletics would be entitled to *all* the benefits set forth in the Bill of Rights. Perhaps most significantly, we gave every scholarship athlete a lifetime degree guarantee that even if they leave IU, for any reason, IU Athletics will pay their tuition to get their undergraduate degree. This groundbreaking Hoosiers for Life program is a fundamental part of who we are, as it is an important, tangible example of our commitment to our students for their entire lives, not just as long as they are eligible to play sports. As of this writing, twenty former students have come back and graduated tuition-free through this program.

And it's not just for the young kids. Ernie Thompson graduated at fifty, and Tim Wilbur is pursuing his degree at age sixty, both as part of the Hoosiers for Life program.

In addition, for the first time ever, we made our scholarships good for four years as opposed to year-to-year scholarships that leave students unsure about their status for the following year. We also committed to detailed, comprehensive academic support; health, safety, and wellness support; athletic support; leadership and life skills development; a culture of trust and respect; a collective voice for students through the Student-Athlete Advisory Committee; and cutting-edge technology. As part of these "big things," we wanted to include a couple of "little things" to help tangibly bring home what we were more broadly trying to do here—as I find "little things" are often good at doing. Thus, the Bill of Rights guarantees *every* student (again from a five-star scholarship basketball player to a walk-on rowing novice) a personally tailored blue blazer with brass IU buttons and candy-striped lining with an interlocking IU logo as well as an iPad with a leather IU Athletics cover (both of which they are allowed to keep). These items, in addition to being highly functional (our academic services team especially loved the iPads, where they could load, for example, specialized academic programming for different learners), helped make special being an IU student participating in intercollegiate athletics *and* let them know they were all an equally important part of the one big team.

The Bill of Rights has become a nationally recognized innovation in the care and development of students participating in intercollegiate athletics. Although it wasn't our goal when we developed the Bill of Rights, it has also become a great recruiting tool for us. Parents often come to campus visits with a copy of it printed from their home computer excited about the commitments we are making to their children, unlike anywhere else in intercollegiate athletics.

* * *

From even before I was athletic director, I was disappointed as a fan in what ironically seemed like a lack of uniformity with our uniforms. After I became athletic director, I became even more disappointed as I discovered that lack of uniformity went beyond our uniforms to the use of our marks, typography, and even how we described ourselves. After years of work trying to get all our uniforms and equipment to be the same red; primarily utilizing a certain set of marks (the IU trident, script Indiana, and candy stripes); having "Indiana" on our uniforms; using stars to represent national championships; and, to underscore our status as the state's flagship university, incorporating our logo in an outline of the state of Indiana, we finally codified in 2018 all this and more in the first-ever Indiana University Department of Intercollegiate Athletics Brand and Uniform Guidelines. Presenting yourself in a cogent, consistent manner is important with any organization, but particularly an athletic department representing its university. While seemingly pedestrian, these elusive guidelines constituted a substantial accomplishment for the department.

* * *

People often perceive that the value of having a lawyer as an athletic director, or as the leader of any organization for that matter, is that he or she has the technical expertise to understand and handle legal matters involving contracts, business deals, litigation and other disputes, Title IX and other legislation, employment matters, and the like. And there is value in that. But I believe the greatest value of having a lawyer lead an organization is that he or she knows how to cut through what doesn't matter to get to what does. This is a skill often taken for granted by lawyers who practice it every day usually working among other lawyers. This was brought home very clearly to me when I left the large law firm of Baker & Daniels where I was working every day mostly with and against lawyers to go to IU's athletic department where, when I started, there were no lawyers on my senior staff.

Nowhere is there more value in "thinking like a lawyer," as described above, than in the critical function of risk management. Every day the reputation of the Athletic Department, and thus the entire university, is put at risk by issues that arise, especially those involving how students are treated and cared for. At least as important as the nature of the issues themselves is how they are handled. It is often, and accurately, observed that athletics isn't the most important room in the university house, but it is the most visible—the front porch, you might say. Lawyers are particularly good at risk management. It's the essence of what we do every day. I was acutely aware that I was the AD only because my predecessor had essentially failed at risk management. I told President McRobbie during my interview that I could not warrant to him that nothing bad would happen under my watch if he made me AD. I told him, in fact, that bad things *would* happen. But I promised him that those things would be handled promptly, professionally, and completely in a way of which he and the university could be proud. Here are my fundamental rules for effective risk management:

## 1. Establish and Communicate Clear expectations

You can't expect your people to behave if you do not clearly establish and communicate to them how you expect them to behave. I believe in the maxim, "If it's important, write it down." This started with our most important and fundamental set of expectations, the Five Priorities, and our bedrock values, which led to the tenets of the Spirit of Indiana: 24 Sports, One Team and the Student-Athlete Bill of Rights, as well as specific policies such as the Sexual Violence Disqualification Policy. We also developed our Importance of Knowing program and Openness and Teamwork Initiative described in more detail below. Importantly, starting in 2015, to reinforce our expectations and document their communication, at the beginning of every calendar year, I sent emails to all staff members, every head coach, and every student participating in intercollegiate athletics setting forth our most important policies and expectations to "make sure all of us know the philosophies, resources, and expectations of the department, even if you may have joined the department after a particular policy or similar communication was adopted and/or circulated.... Please take the time to review this update as you will be held to know and abide by the information set forth and referenced in it."

## 2. Create a Culture of Truthfulness

You can't address risk if you don't know about it. Unless you clearly and consistently communicate to the members of your organization that you want them to tell you about "bad news" (i.e., risk) *and* act like that when they do, too often they won't out of fear of becoming a "shot messenger," that they might somehow get blamed, that you don't really want to know, that you already know and want it to be ignored, or some other reason. Fairly early in my tenure as AD, a "scandal" occurred at Ohio State where football players were trading their gear for tattoos. Head Coach Jim Tressel ultimately lost his job over it. In retrospect, it seems a rather quaint scandal. The next big one involved an out-of-control booster at the University of Miami who was providing football players and recruits with drugs, cash, prostitutes, and other—in the rather antiseptic nomenclature of the NCAA—"improper benefits."

That was when it hit me: although I wasn't smart enough to know what the basis for the next scandal in college athletics would be, it was predictable that it would happen—or at least continue to happen—because good people knew but didn't tell for one of the reasons suggested above or some other reason. With that in mind, I started the Importance of Knowing program through which we repeatedly and clearly communicated to our staff that we wanted to know about any potential rules violations like those that happened at Ohio State and Miami and that not only would they not be in trouble if they "told," they would be in trouble if they didn't. I had thought that Miami was as bad as it could get, and then Penn State happened, where former football coach Jerry Sandusky used his status with its athletic department as a platform from which to sexually abuse young boys. That became our quintessential example of why the Importance of Knowing was so important, and we expanded it from applying just to rules compliance issues to any kind of misbehavior or wrongdoing. We also started the complementary Openness and Teamwork Initiative through which we actively encouraged our staff and students to report any areas of concern.

As a direct result of these programs and related training, a staff member who was casually complained to by a colleague of inappropriate behavior by his boss realized that she needed to tell someone about it, and she did. The complaints were investigated, and the boss was separated from the university. The staff member who reported the inappropriate behavior told us that absent the training, which made clear her duty to report the misbehavior, she likely would have dismissed her colleague's comments as just commiserating among staff. If she had not brought this unacceptable and dangerous situation to light, who knows how long it would have continued and how it ultimately would have adversely impacted her colleague as well as the university.

### 3. When There is an Incident, Get the Facts, Fast

When a risk management matter actually arises and you are shifting to damage control, implement its well-recognized first rule: get all the facts. This can be more challenging than it seems it ought to be. When there is some sort of crisis, it is often the case that initial reports are at best incomplete and sometimes just plain wrong. Unfortunately, as in war, the first casualty of a crisis is often truth. Thus, while it is critical to demand to get the unvarnished facts of the situation as quickly as possible, do not rush to judgment or believe everything you hear, especially early on. Verify the facts to the greatest extent possible under the circumstances before acting, but know you will likely have to act before you have all the information you would like to have. That's okay, but proceed knowing the facts may change as you go along.

## 4. Get the Facts Out, Fast

Particularly in light of the above, don't wait for the perfect understanding of all the facts before reporting it to your boss and other appropriate parties. Bosses don't like surprises. You may have legal obligations to notify other third parties, particularly when dealing with situations potentially involving sexual assault or other personal misconduct. Especially if you work for a public entity, like being the AD at a public university, get the facts out publicly as quickly and completely as you can under the circumstances, even if your ability to do so is limited by employee or student privacy interests. A person who sits on a hot story often gets his behind burnt. It's much better to be publicly forthcoming a little earlier than you would like than be found out by the press or others as you are trying to pursue additional information. If you do comment publicly, steadfastly avoid famous last words (e.g., "We are confident no rules were broken," or "We know he didn't do anything wrong") because facts tend to evolve. People, especially the press, hate uncertainty regarding an incident, and your own people will want assurances "that everything's going to be all right." Unfortunately, until the situation's course has been completely run, everyone will have to live with a little uncertainty.

## 5. Think of What in Six Weeks You Will Have Wished You'd Have Done Now, and Do It

This is my most valuable rule. The problem with these incidents is that we have to deal with them in real time with a constantly evolving understanding of the facts, yet how we handle the incident will be judged with twenty-twenty hindsight after the facts are well established. This calls for some good old-fashioned Ignatian detachment: step back from your initial biases and willingly balance the alternatives carefully without concern for the impact of doing the right thing. Issues come at you fast all day, every day. Sometimes their potential negative implications aren't fully appreciated or described by those bringing them to you for a variety of reasons. Be aware of the "drive-by date stamp" where someone is telling you just enough so they can say they brought it to your attention but not enough to get you wondering whether they have handled it well to this point. Slow down. Ask questions. Trust your instincts. Issues that can bring down the house don't walk in your door with "CRISIS" stamped on their forehead.

As soon as I identify a situation as being one that poses some significant risk to the organization, I go through an exercise where I imagine what would happen if the facts turned out to be as bad as they could be and I did nothing. Then I go back and think if the facts are that bad, what will I have wished in six weeks I had done now, and then I do it. This exercise has proven invaluable to me and led to good, dispassionate decision-making during times when emotions are otherwise often running high. Examples of this include, unfortunately, several instances of asking the University General Counsel's Office and or outside law firms to investigate allegations of inappropriate conduct by department personnel. Always do the right thing, even when no one knows or appreciates that you are and even when the right thing looks to some like the wrong thing.

Similarly, in 2017, we retained Spectrum Collegiate Sports Consulting to conduct an Institutional Control Assessment of IU Athletics as "a comprehensive analysis of departmental policies, operations, and documentation to assess the institution's control over its athletics programs." Lack of institutional control is the most devastating finding the NCAA can make on an athletic department. We believed that this exercise with Spectrum, especially when we were not currently dealing with a particular infraction allegation, would not only be helpful in improving the department's institutional control, but would also be extremely valuable to document the department's successful, significant attention to the issue of institutional control to the NCAA with regard to any future compliance issues.

After a nine-month review, Spectrum provided us a twelve-page report that concluded, in pertinent part, that "Indiana University has high compliance expectations for its employees and staff, which University leadership has established and constantly emphasized. Overall, those high expectations are met. . . . In all, Indiana's culture and practices are sound in institutional control and it operates with the highest compliance expectations." Given that it was prepared by very well-respected third-party professionals who had complete, unfettered access regarding all our compliance matters and functions, the Spectrum Report has been very compelling evidence of IU Athletics' successful ongoing commitment to institutional control.

For similar reasons, also in 2017, we commissioned a comprehensive best practices review of our medical services to students by a team led by Dr. Anikar Chhabra, who was the Director of Sports Medicine at the Mayo Clinic Arizona and the team orthopedic surgeon at Arizona State University, as well as a former intercollegiate basketball player at Harvard. Their 2018 report concluded that our primary care sports staff was excellent, that the culture and collaboration with our outside orthopedic surgeons was good and worked well, that our concussion protocols were well run and up-to-date, and, very importantly, that we were meeting the NCAA standard of medical care.

Also importantly, the consulting physicians reviewed seven deidentified cases where the students involved had complained about their care. Our outside experts found that in every case, the medical services provided met the standard of care. Specifically, the report concluded that "overall, the cases reviewed demonstrated that the physicians are performing appropriate treatments for high-level athletes with no concern." This came in very handy when later a former student-athlete made what we strongly believed were unfounded complaints about his medical care to a prominent, national television sports program. When we were able to show its producer that his case had been previously reviewed by the highly respected Dr. Chhabra, the producer declined to pursue the matter, and we were not included on a broadcast criticizing other universities for the care of some of their students participating in intercollegiate athletics.

# 16. THE COACHES

One of my favorite and most instructive Herman B Wells quotes is this one from his autobiography, *Being Lucky: Reminiscences and Reflections*: "The quality of the faculty is the most important ingredient in the success of the university. Many things can be done to help members of the faculty, but the greatest laboratories, the finest buildings, and the largest salaries will mean little without [people] of absolutely top quality to use them. And so the recruitment and retention of superior faculty members must be the first objective of any administration and must have top priority in the use of the administrator's energy, mind, and body" (Wells 1980, 101–102). For me, coaches were our faculty. Like with Wells and his faculty, while we were working hard on the important business of having great buildings, policies, and the like, coaches would be the most important ingredient in the success of our sports and ultimately the department. All that other stuff could be great, but without high-quality coaches embracing our values, we would simply not be successful on and off the playing fields. I knew our coaches would understandably wonder when I was hired how this lawyer from Indianapolis who never played, coached, or administered intercollegiate athletics could possibly help them in reaching their goals as coaches.

That is why I started working hard even before I actually became athletic director to nurture my relationships with the head coaches. I met with each one individually as well as with them all collectively. As part of those meetings, I learned there was great dissatisfaction with the monthly head coach / athletic director meetings under my predecessor, which were perceived by the coaches as nothing more than lectures and directives from the AD and his senior administrators at the coaches with little, if any, engagement permitted by the coaches. I changed the format of my monthly meetings with the coaches to be just me with my pad and paper mostly listening and learning. In addition, I set weekly office hours every Wednesday as a time any coach could come see me with a question or concern or just to shoot the breeze. This was in response to concerns raised during my preemployment meetings with coaches that my predecessor played favorites among coaches and never interacted with more than two or three of them. I also proactively set regular meetings with the head coaches of men's basketball, women's basketball, football, and volleyball as our highest-profile men's and women's sports.

In all these meetings, I looked for opportunities to quickly and positively address their questions, concerns, and requests or to tell them why I couldn't so they would know I hadn't just ignored them. Over time, I feel as though I earned their trust, even when I had to tell them things they didn't want to hear.

I learned a great deal from working with our coaches. Much of what I've learned is sprinkled throughout these pages, but there are some specific insights that have been particularly useful to me, and I hope they might be useful to you as well. First, many coaches would tell me that they would teach some variation of the following maxim with their students: "Prepare intensely and methodically, but when the moment to perform comes, trust your preparation and just let go." I specifically remember our three-time All-American pole vaulter Vera Neuenswander telling me about being in a slump. She would put a lot of pressure on herself and overthink her mechanics, technique, and cues while she was jumping. Then, in her last chance to qualify for the Olympic trials, she affirmatively decided to trust her training, not think about what she was doing, and just allow herself to be in "that flow state." She cleared 14.9 and earned an automatic qualification for the trials. Her coach, Ron Helmer, had encouraged her to do just what she did: trust her training and compete in the moment. Ron is one of our very best and most consistently successful coaches. He exudes the confidence and wisdom of someone who has been a college coach for nearly thirty years. Ron would tell his athletes, "You don't have to feel your best to do your best. Don't build in excuses to fail. Succeed even in the face of perceived adversities." Like many of us, athletes can fall into a trap of doing exactly that, building in potential excuses in case they fail, which can become a self-fulfilling prophecy: I had a bad week of practice; I didn't sleep well last night; my throat's sore; I drew a bad lane. Coach Helmer shares with his athletes example after example where their peers overcame such challenges to set personal bests and win races.

These precepts about trusting your preparation and not building in excuses have been profoundly emancipating for me. I am an overpreparer by nature, and the first one gives me permission, after I have rigorously prepared, just to let it go, trust my preparation, and have fun in my presentation, interview, or whatever it is. A master at building in excuses in case I fail or otherwise don't meet my own high expectations, I have learned from Ron's second maxim that I can succeed in spite of them and that therefore they really don't matter and can be safely and productively ignored. This all reminded me of an observation Bart Peterson once made to me when he was mayor: "Nobody cares about your excuses; they only care about your performance." He went on to specify that nobody knows or cares if you had an argument with your wife this morning or that you are battling diarrhea; they just know whether you seemed engaging, comfortable, and knowledgeable in your live TV interview. I took his point to be similar to Ron's, that since those excuses won't really "excuse" a poor performance because nobody will ever know or care about them, they are ultimately useless to you; you might as well forget them and know you just have to perform. Although perhaps obvious to some, this idea that you don't have to feel your best to do your best I believe has significantly improved my performances and my state of mind in preparing for and executing them.

Another very useful maxim I first heard from my coaches is this: "The temptation to quit will be greatest just before you are about to succeed." Football Coach Tom Allen would bring this to life by asking his players when people quit running a marathon. Here are the answers: (1) the fewest quit in the first mile; (2) the second fewest quit in the last mile; and (3) the most quit in the twentieth mile—after they have already completed over three-quarters of the race! He encourages his players not to fall into this trap of quitting because you are physically and mentally drained and can't see the finish line; rather, remember how far you have come and your vision for success to keep going.

Of course, it's not all inspiration, roses, and lollipops with our coaches. People in their occupations are used to being the kings or queens of their programs, with little dissent or challenging views coming from their staffs and certainly not their students, at least traditionally. In this environment, I am sometimes the only one who can tell them the truth, especially things they don't want to hear. It's a very tricky relationship in which the AD's all-in support in a very volatile, often very public endeavor is critical yet, behind the scenes, it is incumbent on the AD to advise the coach when you think he or she is making a mistake or otherwise needs to improve.

Unfortunately, sometimes, for various reasons, I would get to the point where I felt that I had to fire a coach. It is the worst part of the job. Sometimes they make it comparatively easy by lying, stealing, physically and/or verbally abusing a staff member, or violating a direct, written prohibition. Unfortunately, I dealt with all of these. The tougher ones are when you are dealing with the more nebulous area of competitive performance. What's the standard (which fairly varies from sport to sport given our tradition, expectation, and competition)? What did he or she inherit? What's the trajectory? How much time do you give? What is the role of injuries or other matters outside of their control? What are the likely alternatives? Even as you are asking yourself these questions, which any responsible AD needs to do under appropriate circumstances, for the good of the program, your coach is your coach until he or she isn't. The public often doesn't understand how you can publicly stand behind your coach when there are so many seemingly obvious shortcomings, and they can assume you are just oblivious. Coaches often don't understand how you can be working like crazy to support them right up until you feel you have to make a change, and they can assume you are just duplicitous. Such is the lot of the AD.

I never liked making a coaching change. Barbara could tell when I was contemplating one because I would always lose weight from the stress. Of course, as hard as it is on me, it's much harder on them, so I don't seek any sympathy on that score. I learned in public service that I didn't owe my loyalty to my colleagues or other state employees but rather to what was right for the citizens of Indiana. Similarly, in athletics I felt that I didn't owe my loyalty to my coaches or other department staff but rather to what was right for Indiana University. Of our nineteen coaches, by the time I left IU, I had hired fifteen of them, and in a few of those cases, I unfortunately was on my second or third go-around. I think this reflects that although I didn't like it, I didn't shirk from my responsibility to walk up to changes and make them when I felt they needed to be made in the best interest of a program and the department. I am very proud of the cadre of head coaches we recruited and retained, and I believe that outstanding faculty is well positioned to lead us into a new golden age of IU Athletics.

I'm not going to revisit all the coach goings and comings, but it probably wouldn't be a fair book if I didn't touch upon just a few.

* * *

My first coaching change was with one of our most successful and celebrated programs just a few weeks after I was hired. Mike Freitag was the head coach of our men's soccer team. He played for legendary coach Jerry

Yeagley and was Jerry's handpicked successor. He won a national championship in his first year as head coach. He was named Big Ten Coach of the Year multiple times. He had just been to the Sweet Sixteen of the NCAA tournament. He is clearly a very good soccer coach. He is also a wonderful person whom I liked very much. So how could I be contemplating a change? Well, Mike's senior class was the first in IU men's soccer history not to make a College Cup, soccer's Final Four. As well as Mike had done, for this program we needed to do better, so I decided I needed to move on from Mike.

Then there was the matter of Todd Yeagley, who was one of our best players of all time and the son of our legendary coach. He had been an assistant to Mike until the year before when Wisconsin hired him away to be their head coach. Many thought that Todd had been a big part of the success that Mike was able to have. Todd had done well in his first year at Wisconsin, and I was concerned that Todd was going to build a powerhouse at Wisconsin, potentially diluting the incredible power of our men's soccer tradition and alumni. So I decided to pursue him as Mike's successor. It has worked out well. While I was at IU, Todd was named Conference Coach of the Year three times as well as the National Coach of the Year and led us to six conference titles, three College Cups, and the national championship in 2012, earning us a memorable trip to the White House to be congratulated by President Obama.

* * *

When I interviewed with the AD search committee, rebuilding the football program was a cornerstone of my presentation. At the time, IU football was historically among the least successful programs in the nation. Its overall winning percentage was the worst among all Power Five conference schools, it had been to only one bowl game in the last fifteen years, and its forty-year Rose Bowl drought was exceeded by only Minnesota's forty-seven-year absence among Big Ten programs. Herman Wells famously said that Indiana University should be excellent in all its endeavors. We were not excellent in football, and, in my view, we needed to be for three basic reasons. First, fair or not, the quality of your football team reflects disproportionately on the quality of your institution. Second, our badly performing football team was reflected in historically poor attendance, which provided a profound opportunity to dramatically increase attendance and revenue for the benefit of the football program and the entire department. Third, I believe that if attending football games is part of an undergraduate's IU experience, he or she is much more likely to stay connected to the university as an alumnus. Thus, I believed that the stakes for football at IU could not have been higher, providing us our biggest opportunity to turn IU Athletics around.

I further believed that developing IU football into an excellent program would require two things: (1) consistency of great leadership; and (2) ongoing substantial investments. When I was hired, the average tenure of the head football coach at Indiana since Bill Mallory had been fired was three years. You can't build a football program like that. Most importantly, it kills you in recruiting. The key to winning is starting to stack respectable, and then outstanding, recruiting classes on top of each other; you can't do that if you keep changing the head coach. Hand in hand with consistency of great leadership is the necessity for ongoing substantial investments. When I got back to IU as athletic director, Memorial Stadium still consisted of two grandstands facing each other (the north end zone enclosure was started but not fully paid for), not unlike a Mid-American Conference school or even a 6A high school, but certainly not a Big Ten school. Moreover, our football coaches' salaries ranked at the bottom of the Big Ten, not even close to the next-lowest coaches.

Bill Lynch was the coach when I got there. He is a great person *and* a great football coach. He had inherited, through no fault of his own, an almost impossible situation by coaching the team as an interim head coach while Terry Hoeppner fought his valiant fight against brain cancer, which he ultimately lost during the 2007 season. Bill did a masterful job of leading his team that year under the worst of circumstances to IU's first bowl game in thirteen years, with a 7–6 record (3–5 in the Big Ten). He was named head coach in his own right for the 2008 season, but the uncertainty about Coach Hoeppner's health had really taken a toll on recruiting, and the Hoosiers found themselves undermanned, falling to 3–9 (1–7 Big Ten).

When I got to IU for the 2009 season, under the circumstances, I had my doubts as to whether Bill would be able to get us where we wanted to go. But I believed he deserved to have the opportunity to try, particularly given that he had just completed the first year of a four-year contract given to him by my predecessor. Thus, after meeting with Bill, and before I even actually became AD, I publicly announced that Bill would continue to be our head coach, quieting speculation that there might be a change after Purdue drubbed us 62–10 in the 2008 Old Oaken Bucket, our annual rivalry game. One of my biggest concerns was Bill's staff, many of whom were young carryovers from Coach Hoeppner's Miami of Ohio staff, which had been decimated from his predecessor's move to Northwestern.

I offered Bill to fund any replacements he might want to make to his staff, but he was loyal to them and didn't want to make any changes. After the 2010 season, with one year left on his contract, I had to decide whether Bill should continue to lead our program. Having failed to make a bowl game in his first two years of my tenure, and being embarrassed at Wisconsin 83–20, I believed Bill just wasn't going to be able to turn the hand he was dealt into a winner. I decided to make a change.

I quickly settled on Kevin Wilson as the replacement for Bill. Kevin seemed to have all the predictors for success. He had been an innovative and successful offensive coordinator winning at traditional nonpower Midwest football programs Miami of Ohio and Northwestern, as well as at traditional national power football program Oklahoma. He had won the Frank Broyles Award for the best assistant football coach in the country. He was widely regarded as an offensive football genius. He had worked for two of the most highly respected, and reportedly grounded, head football coaches in the country, Randy Walker and Bob Stoops. When I met him, he seemed confident yet unassuming and very knowledgeable about football, with a specific plan about how he would win at Indiana. His references all checked out.

When Kevin got to campus, he had a few issues I attributed to the growing pains of becoming a head coach, exacerbated by stress from being separated from his family, who stayed in Oklahoma to finish the school year. I sought out advice from my friend and mentor Bill Polian on whether he thought Kevin would be able to address his issues. He told me most people don't change, but smart people can. Kevin is clearly very smart, and I believed he wanted to and would.

After winning just one game in his first season in 2011, Kevin started getting the program going in the right direction through improved recruiting, strong player development, and great offensive scheme. He won four games in 2012, five in 2013, four in 2014, and then six in 2015—including our third straight Bucket win over Purdue—the first three-peat in more than fifty years, qualifying for just our second bowl game in twenty-two years. Still, I almost made a change after that season. Although I was generally pleased with our on-field progress, I had continuing concerns about Kevin's ability to lead the program and his players the way I expected them to be led and thus facilitate consistent winning. In fact, after the 2015 season, I retained the same outside headhunter who had helped with the search that originally led to Kevin in 2010 to explore options for replacing him. He had active conversations on my behalf with a number of credible candidates.

In the end, after talking to Kevin about my off-field concerns and receiving what I felt were (and still feel were!) sincere assurances that he would positively address them, I concluded to give him a new six-year contract. Importantly, and to the chagrin of Kevin and his agent, it was purposefully a contract that I could terminate under terms very favorable for IU. I was very clear with Kevin about my motivation for doing so: "Kevin, I want you to feel my hot breath on your neck about leading this program the way you know I want it to be led." Unfortunately, it wasn't successful.

On December 1, 2016, three days after our school-record-tying fourth-straight regular-season-ending victory over Purdue, qualifying us for back-to-back bowl appearances for the first time in twenty-five years, I announced that I had accepted Kevin's resignation, effective immediately, "based upon philosophical differences as to the leadership of the football program." It wasn't about the performance of the football team, which I viewed as quite positive and heading in the right direction. It boiled down to leadership. I concluded that we weren't on the same page, and as the athletic director, I had to make a call. I spoke at the press conference announcing Kevin's resignation:

> I'm an IU guy. I grew up in Indiana. I went to school at Indiana. My mom went to school at Indiana. My kids went to school at Indiana. I have a senior here at Indiana. And my focus is Indiana. So what might be okay at other places, what might be okay in an industry, isn't necessarily okay here. That doesn't make me right or wrong, but I can tell you that I came at this earnestly and with the best interest of Indiana University at heart. And I'll tell you that I'm proud to be part of an institution that puts doing what it thinks is the right thing ahead of competitive success, and I think we've had competitive success the last couple of years in football.

Always do the right thing, even when no one knows or appreciates that you are and even when the right thing looks to some like the wrong thing.

I immediately turned to Tom Allen, Kevin's defensive coordinator, to succeed Kevin as the head coach. In fact, I was able to announce hiring Tom as Kevin's permanent replacement in the same press conference that I announced Kevin's resignation. I had helped Kevin recruit Tom and had become very impressed with his coaching and his ability to lead young men. I had already concluded that if Kevin moved on (which, if it happened, I had assumed would be him being hired away as a result of his success at Indiana), I would hire Tom as the head coach. Having taken a hard look at the football coach marketplace in 2015 when I almost moved on from Kevin also helped me be comfortable hiring Tom without a national search. I didn't care that hiring Tom wouldn't "win the press conference," and in fact it was almost universally criticized. I had seen him up close and had great confidence in him.

Tom won five games in each of his first two years and in each of them had a chance for a bowl-qualifying sixth in the season finales against Purdue but came up a little short each time. Contrary to the feelings of some, I found these first two seasons encouraging, particularly for a first-time head college football coach. I could see how Tom was building a great culture, improving recruiting, and developing his players.

In Tom's third year as IU head coach, my last at Indiana, Indiana football truly broke through. The turning point for the season, and perhaps the program, came when we went to play Nebraska at Lincoln on October 26, 2019. IU had not beaten Nebraska in sixty years. In addition, Nebraska's head coach, Scott Frost, at a meeting at the annual Fiesta Summit in Scottsdale, Arizona, in May 2018—which included every Big Ten athletic director and head football coach along with a substantial number of Big Ten staff members—openly and repeatedly complained that the conference's projected future schedules were unfair to Nebraska because Nebraska did not get to play Indiana enough. Coach Frost had only recently been hired by Nebraska, his alma mater, and this was his first Big Ten meeting. Tom and I were sitting together just a few feet from Coach Frost as he was making his comments about Indiana. Although I was boiling, I felt there wasn't anything I could say because the facts were that Nebraska had our number. For better or worse, I believe these kind of disputes can only be resolved on the field of play. Legendary Pittsburgh Steeler Coach Chuck Noll once said, "The critics are always right. The only way you shut them up is by winning."

Knowing that we next played Nebraska in two years there, I slid a piece of paper over to Tom: "The only way to shut this guy up is to beat their ass in Lincoln." Tom quietly nodded to me and stuck the note in his folder.

I confess to having silently seethed about that for the following seventeen months. Finally, the week of the Nebraska game arrived. We came into the game at 5–2 with the opportunity to clinch a bowl berth for the first time in the Tom Allen era. Nebraska was 4–3 coming off Coach Frost's much-anticipated but disappointing inaugural Nebraska season. I asked Tom if I could speak to the entire team, something I hadn't done all year and had been saving for this week. The day before the game, I walked into the team room, and Tom introduced me. I looked at the 120 or so players sitting up straight, looking at me intently. I reminded them how Tom loved them and always had their backs. Then I told them that tomorrow I wanted *them* to have *Tom's* back. I shared what Scott Frost had said about Indiana football to Tom's face in front of all the other head football coaches and ADs in the Big Ten Conference that day in Scottsdale. I told them what I wrote on that piece of paper that I had slid over to Tom. I finished by telling them that we didn't need to play perfect to beat this team, we just needed to play with grit, toughness, and resilience, and that when the final gun went off, we'd have Coach's back and make Scott Frost wish he never had to play Indiana again. My guys went crazy.

On gameday, one of my favorite players, wide receiver Whop Philyor, got off the bus with a Chucky doll because the Hoosiers "were going to be scary." The coaches were not pleased, but that's Whop, and in fairness, it was Halloween week. The team fed off his attitude and his play. Nebraska got off to a fast start, throwing everything at us, including a bunch of early trick plays. They even wore their black jerseys, which I took as an additional insult because you don't break out your iconic special jersey in front of your home fans unless you are confident you are going to win. They came to win, and we were down 14–3 early. It looked as though it might be another long day against the Cornhuskers. But our guys were full of fight. They wouldn't back down. They were not to be denied, especially Whop, who played like a man possessed (like Chucky?) with fourteen catches for 178 yards. When the clock hit double zero, we won 38–31, were bowl eligible, and beat Nebraska for the first time in sixty years—and on their home field to boot in front of their ninety thousand fans. In the locker room after the game, I presented the game ball to Tom. Later, standing on the airport tarmac before boarding the team plane, I told a reporter in a phone interview that the win "was particularly gratifying, particularly knowing Nebraska's staff had no respect for our program."

Whop simply, and accurately, told the media: "They got what they wanted." Or at least what they thought they wanted. I told Whop to bring along Chucky anytime.

In my last year as AD, Indiana football had its best regular season in twenty-six years. Its eight wins tied for the third most in program history and was just one shy of the school record previously set by the 1945 and 1967 Big Ten championship teams. It also constituted its first winning Big Ten season in twenty-six years and only sixth in the last fifty years. Again, we beat Nebraska for the first time in sixty years and were ranked nationally for the first time in twenty-five years. We won our fifth Old Oaken Bucket in seven years (the sixth of the decade, the most since the 1940s) and qualified for just our fourth bowl game in twenty-five years. Three of those four were in just the last five years. We earned our first-ever Florida bowl trip, appearing in the Gator Bowl. Tom had more wins by far in his first three years as IU's football coach (eighteen) than any other coach in IU football history. I'm proud that one of my last significant acts as athletic director was to give Tom a well-earned new seven-year contract.

* * *

While the IU football program had struggled for more than a century before I arrived, the IU men's basketball program's history was profoundly different. With five national championships and twenty Big Ten titles (at the time I was hired), the program is one of the nation's blue bloods. But for all IU's historical success, the program was in a very different position in 2009. In November 2008, the NCAA Committee on Infractions concluded its investigation into the program and the recruiting violations committed by former coach Kelvin Sampson. The NCAA ultimately accepted IU's self-imposed penalties that included, among other things, a three-year probation.

If football provided the biggest opportunity to turn IU Athletics around, men's basketball provided its most important. No sport—maybe nothing at all—is more meaningful in the state of Indiana than basketball, and that is epitomized by the illustrious tradition and passionate fan base of Indiana University men's basketball. IU basketball fans rightfully expect greatness, and everything is better not only at Indiana University but all around the state when IU basketball is winning.

My predecessor hired Tom Crean shortly before he was fired himself, so the second half of Tom's first season was during my first year as AD. It was the first year after the Kelvin Sampson major infractions case, which had the effect of wiping the team out. All Sampson's productive players left one way or another, and Tom was forced to bring in baseball players and kids off the intramural teams. The program was at its lowest point in history. That was not what Tom had expected or what he had signed up for in leaving a very successful tenure at Marquette.

Shortly after I arrived back at IU as AD, Tom said to me that he had found IU basketball to be only an illusion of its public perception as a well-resourced, first-class college basketball program. Because, as I soon discovered, he wasn't wrong about that, I worked hard during his tenure—and, as it turns out, beyond—to ensure that we dedicated the tens of millions of dollars in resources necessary to support an elite basketball program, including funding and completing the basketball development facility, which became Cook Hall; renovating and modernizing what became Simon Skjodt Assembly Hall; and substantially increasing our operational investments in recruiting, team travel, assistant coaches, other staff, and the like. Given its significance to the department, the university, and the state, Indiana University men's basketball could not, and did not, want for any resource.

Through sheer force of will, Tom did an amazing job of righting the listing ship he had inherited. I don't think there's another coach in the country with the skill set and personality to take us from how bad we were to how good we got. After three understandably very challenging years given what he had been left, in 2011–2012, Tom had us back into the NCAA tournament with a 27–9 record and a Sweet Sixteen appearance. Of course, that was also the season of the "Wat Shot," where Christian Watford's buzzer-beating three-pointer took down number-one-ranked Kentucky and set off pandemonium in Assembly Hall, Nick's, and all across Hoosier Nation. Indiana basketball changed in that instant. Although of course one regular-season win doesn't make a season, let alone a program, it did show that Indiana basketball was back to being nationally relevant, even if we had a long way to go to get all the way back to where we wanted to be.

After the great steps forward that season, I concluded we'd extend Tom's contract, particularly given the success he was having recruiting—including quality Indiana kids—as well as what seemed to be great prospects for the 2012–2013 season. The universal optimism for Tom and the program was so strong that I took a page out of our announcement of the Colts deal to announce Tom's new contract from the floor of Assembly Hall to the crowd before a game. They went wild! That 2013 team was ranked as the number one team in the country for thirteen weeks and was the number one seed in the NCAA tournament, even picked to win it all by President Obama in his official bracket. Unfortunately, we were upset by Syracuse in the Sweet Sixteen. Given the amazing success and promise of that team, it was a devastating loss for them and all of Hoosier Nation, including me and Tom.

Of course, Tom had much success during his tenure. He won two outright Big Ten titles and was named Conference Coach of the Year. He was the third-winningest coach in Indiana basketball history. He recruited and developed great "under the radar" players like Victor Oladipo, OG Anunoby, and Juwan Morgan, as well as more heralded guys like Yogi Ferrell, Cody Zeller, Noah Vonleh, and Thomas Bryant, all of whom are currently playing in the NBA. Tom is a good and giving man who extended many, many quiet kindnesses to Hoosiers across the state, including me and my family. He took my dying friend Bobby Clifford under his wing, welcomed him into postgame locker rooms, visited him at his home multiple times, and attended his funeral. In 2016, our son George was making a college decision between IU and Michigan. As he was deciding, we attended the IU versus Michigan regular-season finale basketball game at Crisler Arena. IU won in thrilling fashion, and by so doing won the Big Ten championship outright. In the locker room afterward, Victor Oladipo hugged George and asked, "Are you ready to commit now?" I had no doubt he did so at the request of Tom Crean.

Notwithstanding the success Tom had (including the second Big Ten title and being named Big Ten Coach of the Year just the year before), as the 2016–2017 season wore on, I knew I was heading toward a crossroad about Tom and the program's future. At the end of the season, he would have only three years left on his contract. I felt as though I needed to make one of three decisions: (1) extend his contract; (2) let him continue to coach without a contract extension; or (3) make a change. I was very open with Tom about these options. After our exit from the Big Ten tournament, I discussed them with him on three consecutive days, the last two in person. I told him at each meeting that an extension was unlikely given the team's performance that year; that I was open to having him go forward without a contract extension, but I feared that would make him "dead man walking" with every misstep and setback blown out of proportion; and that, while I didn't want to fire him, that was a possibility. They were good, positive conversations. Tom was relaxed and nondefensive. To his great credit, although Tom was understandably advocating for an extension, he was willing to proceed without one. He was willing to take the potential heat, and he believed he could win. Of course, in basketball-crazy Indiana, Tom's future was a major topic of discussion with the media, bloggers, social media, fans, and others weighing in with their views. Our trustees even expressed their views to me, which was fine given that Board Chair Jim Morris and President McRobbie made clear to me and the board that this would be my decision. I'll always be grateful to them for that. There was public speculation that unnamed "major donors" had it in for Tom and were pressuring me to fire him. That was just made up.

I told Tom I would make my decision soon after our last tournament game because I didn't want him to be twisting in the breeze with no decision about his future. We were playing in the National Invitation Tournament, on the road for the first game because I didn't think we should play at home during spring break without our students there. That was a mistake by the way, and I absolutely own it. That Tom wanted to play on the road does not make it any less my responsibility or my decision. In any event, as I got on a plane to fly to Atlanta for our game against Georgia Tech on March 14, I had tentatively decided on option two—to let Tom coach the next year, but without an extension. In retrospect, I see that my view at that time was driven more by my appreciation for all that Tom had done, and recently done, for the program than my honest assessment of his ability to meet my admittedly ambitious expectations for the program, which I had repeatedly shared with Tom and the public: to perennially contend for and win multiple Big Ten championships, regularly go deep into the NCAA tournament, and hang a sixth national championship banner.

After we lost to Georgia Tech, Barbara hugged Tom's wife, Joanie, and told her they were going to be fine. At that moment, we both thought they were.

We flew back from Atlanta the next day, and I went to my office to think quietly and deliberately through my final decision about Tom. The more I thought about it, the more I felt, if I was being honest with myself, that for the good of the program I needed to make a change. In that moment of truth, I came to grips with my reluctant, but ultimately confident, conclusion that long term, Tom was not going to be able meet the clear expectations I had for Indiana basketball. I didn't see this as turning up my nose at the success Tom had been able to produce. If I had been optimistic about a future with Tom, I would have seen these successes as positive and acceptable building blocks. Nor was my conclusion driven by the disappointing season we had just completed. I think it is dangerous, and often misguided, for an AD to treat any particular season (or even a game, as sometime seems to happen) as make-or-break for a coach. Rather, my decision to make a change was based on my dispassionate overall evaluation of Tom's nine years as our head coach and how I perceived that would translate into the program going forward. I also could not ignore my belief that the team would not be well positioned to compete successfully the following season. I, accurately as it turned out, suspected our best three players would go pro. We couldn't get to the NCAA even with those pros, although in fairness, one of our best players, OG Anunoby, did miss several games due to injury. How bad would we be with none of those players in any games the next year? And if we did have a bad year with Tom at the helm, what good in the end would that additional year do him? At the end of that season, I'd almost certainly have to fire him anyway. It could be a very ugly season for Tom and the program with some of our fans who were already a bit restless. How far could I risk the program going down (even out of respect for what Tom had done for it) before I'd be facilitating it being even harder to rebuild? To his great credit, Tom was willing to move forward without an extension and risk the "dead man walking" scenario, but in the end, I wasn't. Even though I appreciated all the many good things Tom did for Indiana basketball and did not want to fire him, I knew that's what I needed to do, and I did it.

Firing Tom completed separating from my two power coaches in just one hundred days, something I never expected to have to do, and it took a toll on me. Many had speculated that after Kevin departed, I wouldn't have it in me to fire Tom, and they were almost right.

There was an unbelievable amount of interest and speculation as to who the new coach would be. I would say it was a frenzy. With the local sports media, and to a certain extent the national sports media, there was a fixation on who our next coach was going to be. People were monitoring tail numbers on private planes flying in and out of Bloomington. My favorite were the erroneous sightings of Billy Donovan and his wife touring Bloomington and looking at homes, which led to hilarious memes of them clearly superimposed at Bloomington landmarks, including in Showalter Fountain!

I'm cynical about search firms, but given the stakes, I hired one for the limited purposes of making contacts with and doing background due diligence on my potential candidates. I would be working off my list, and I wasn't particularly interested in who was on theirs. It wasn't anything against this particular search firm—they did a good job for us. I'm just inherently skeptical—given the nature of their business—of why they may be advocating for a particular candidate and whether what I tell them stays completely confidential. I did talk candidly to dozens of former IU players, those who reached out to me and many more whom I reached out to on my own, about what, or who, I should be looking for in a coach. This included telephone interviews with several who were personally interested in being considered for the job. I also reached out to many other prominent and knowledgeable basketball people to get their advice.

I quickly had a list of about ten guys, about half "above the line" I thought would be excellent, with the balance being guys I thought would be very solid. Archie Miller started above the line and quickly moved to the top. I liked that he was a proven winner, recruiter, and player developer at Dayton. While young, he already had broad, deep, and impressive coaching experience and came from a great coaching tree. He had been a tough-as-nails sharp-shooting five-foot-nine point guard in the Atlantic Coast Conference. He was a lunch bucket, midwestern-type guy. His dad was a legendary high school coach, and his brother was a very successful Power Five head coach. I liked his "defense first" mentality, which, combined with his commitment to toughness and rebounding, would make us tough to beat night in and night out.

I called Archie, and at the end of our very positive telephone interview, I told him I would like to meet with him in person. I figured we could just meet in Richmond, Indiana, about halfway between Bloomington and Dayton. Then I found out he was in Palo Alto with his extended family for his brother's NCAA tournament game. I didn't want to interrupt his trip, so I told Archie that we'd just get together after he got back, which would depend on if or when Arizona lost. As I thought more about it, I knew how crazy the environment was and how many things could go wrong. So I called Archie back and asked him if he'd meet me at the San Francisco airport if Deputy AD Scott Dolson (who also oversaw men's basketball) and I flew out to talk with him. He said that wasn't necessary, but he ultimately agreed. Before he hung up, I said, "Archie, if you knew how much I hate to fly, you would know how serious I am about you being the next coach at IU."

We had a great meeting. It was candid and conversational. Archie was everything and more that I had learned about him through my objective research of his record and the very strong reviews I had received from knowledgeable basketball people. Importantly, he expressly and enthusiastically embraced the high expectations I had laid out to him for our program: to perennially contend for and win multiple Big Ten championships, regularly go deep into the NCAA tournament, and hang a sixth national championship banner. Archie brought his delightful wife, Morgan, which Scott and I took as a good sign that he was seriously interested. Archie had been highly sought after for bigger coaching jobs for several seasons, but he had refused even to talk to any other schools (including his alma mater, North Carolina State) until us. He had a great job at a school that was making basketball a centerpiece of not only its athletic department but the school as a whole, making lots of money, and enjoying great success. He was the clear number one choice for me and Scott.

Of course, I had kept President McRobbie updated on the progress of the search and let him know I intended to offer the job to Archie. It was not in the form of a recommendation, as I believe best practices as well as university and conference policies on institutional control make hiring coaches a decision for athletic directors, not presidents or boards of trustees. If ADs do a bad job of hiring and firing, then presidents should fire them (not do their jobs for them by selecting the coaches themselves). Similarly, if presidents do a bad job of overseeing athletic directors, boards of trustees should fire the president (not do his or her job by directly overseeing the athletic director or, even worse, trying to hire the coach directly). Michael understood and embraced this. Of course, as I wanted him to, he asked a lot of great questions and challenged me on important decisions such as hiring Archie (or firing Tom for that matter), but at the end of the day, he made it clear that those were my decisions, and he accepted my decision to pursue hiring Archie.

All that was left was to finalize the business deal with Archie, which he disarmingly told me he wouldn't let be a problem with his agent or otherwise. It was not widely known that Archie was actually making more money at Dayton than Tom had been making at IU. Archie agreed to take a pay cut to come to IU not because I wasn't willing to pay him more, but because I felt it wouldn't be in his interest to come into the conference making more than other more established coaches who had already had substantial success. Although it was neither my goal nor expectation to "win the press conference" with Archie, his hiring was generally very well received by the pundits and the public, certainly better than Tom Allen's had been!

In any event, under Archie, we continued to make the investments we had started under Tom to support an elite basketball program, including a strong assistant coach and staff salary pool, investing millions of dollars to upgrade our locker rooms and team centers in both Simon Skjodt Assembly Hall and Cook Hall, and investing more in recruiting than any other program in the country. While I was publicly criticized for this last point in particular, as I told the *Indianapolis Star* on August 20, 2019, "I certainly make no apologies for supporting our basketball program at an elite level to help it meet the elite expectations we've very publicly set for it."

After a predictably challenging first year inheriting a non-NCAA tournament team minus its three best players, Archie was probably one win away from qualifying for the NCAA tournament in his second year—not an end goal in itself but what would have been a mark of progress for the program's development. In year three, the program defeated five top-twenty teams (fourth most in the country), and had the NCAA tournament not been canceled as a result of the COVID-19 pandemic, the Hoosiers clearly would have had their name called on Selection Sunday. Unfortunately, the pandemic denied the players not only the reward of playing in the tournament but also the springboard that would have provided for the following season. Through my last three years as AD, Archie had done what he said he would do in recruiting: recruit "inside out," meaning start with getting the best players from the state of Indiana before moving out into the Big Ten geographic footprint and ultimately nationally. In his first three years at IU, Archie successfully recruited three straight Indiana Mr. Basketballs, a first in Indiana basketball's distinguished history. If Khristian Lander hadn't enrolled a year early, Archie may well have had four Mr. Basketballs in a row.

As I retired from IU, I was at peace knowing that we had aggressively and consistently made the type of investments and other decisions we believed would return Indiana University men's basketball to elite status. I was disappointed, however, that I would be leaving before we got there.

* * *

I saw Indiana women's basketball as a real conundrum. For all the historic success and national impact of the men's program, the women's program never seemed able to get on track, notwithstanding having at least some of the same benefits enjoyed by the men's team, including being located in a basketball-mad state with great players and playing in one of the most iconic arenas in college basketball. The women's program, along with the men's, had more recently benefited from the completion of Cook Hall, a state-of-the-art basketball practice and development facility equally split between the two programs. Later the two programs would also benefit from the renovation of what would ultimately be renamed Simon Skjodt Assembly Hall, after philanthropist Cindy Simon Skjodt, whose gift made the renovation possible and made her a role model and hero for all our women athletes, especially the basketball players.

When I arrived in Bloomington as AD, the fairly new head coach was a wonderful woman, Felicia Leggett-Jack, who had been a star player at Syracuse. Felicia had replaced Purdue alumna Sharon Versyp, who had successfully coached IU for just one year before leaving for her alma mater, where, as of this writing, she is still coaching. Felicia is a delightful, charismatic, impressive person who represented Indiana University very well, and I thought she would be able to lead us where we wanted to go with women's basketball. Unfortunately, I ultimately concluded, based on the team's performance and recruiting, that wouldn't be the case, and I terminated her contract. When I told Felicia, she immediately stuck out her hand with her typical class and optimism to shake and thanked me for the opportunity she had been given. She was quickly hired to be the head coach at Buffalo, where, as of this writing, she is having great success. I am very happy for her.

In looking for Felicia's successor, I fairly quickly homed in on the extraordinarily successful and talented coach at Bowling Green University, Curt Miller. Legendary Purdue University and WNBA Indiana Fever coach Lin Dunn reportedly said of the hire, "Wow! IU just said it's serious about women's basketball. Watch out!" Through two seasons, Curt did an excellent job of building the program, including recruiting outstanding players. Ultimately, on July 25, 2014, right before the 2014–2015 season was set to begin, Curt announced that he was resigning for personal health and family reasons.

Given how incredibly close we were to starting our new season, I had to move very quickly. I soon settled on Indiana State Head Coach Teri Moren to replace Curt. Things were going so fast that I actually offered the job to Teri over the phone while she was with her Indiana State team on a layover in Miami on their way to Costa Rica for a foreign tour. Teri was exactly whom we needed. She is a native of Seymour in Southern Indiana. She was an Indiana High School All-Star. To me, she is a classic example of the Indiana girls who should have gone to IU but because of the dismal state of our program went elsewhere, too often, as in Teri's case, to Purdue. She played there for Coach Dunn, winning a Big Ten title. She went on to be the head coach at the University of Indianapolis and then Indiana State. She was known as a hard worker, strong recruiter, and a savvy, demanding coach, but one who earnestly cared about her players. I saw in her the quiet confidence and fiery competitiveness that I thought we needed to be successful.

During our original contract discussions, I was feeling once burned and twice shy about losing a Purdue alum women's basketball coach back to Purdue after what had happened with Sharon Versyp, so I asked Teri if she would be willing to commit to never leaving for Purdue. I knew if she did go to Purdue, I would look like the biggest sucker in the world. I must confess it then seemed unlikely that Teri would ever be coveted by Purdue to replace Sharon, given, at the point in time that I hired Teri, Purdue had gone 13–3 against Indiana since Versyp had gone back to Purdue as head coach. In any event, at my request, Teri specifically assured me she would stay at Indiana over Purdue. So I said, "Then you won't mind if I put a provision in your contract that if you go to Purdue you owe IU ten million dollars?" She later told me she thought I was kidding. I wasn't. It's still there in the new contract, and it doesn't seem so outlandish anymore.

While I was at IU, Teri turned the tide against Purdue, going 8–4 versus Sharon's Boilers, including 6–1 over their last seven games, which IU won by an average of 14 points. We won the WNIT championship in 2018 in front of record-setting home crowds. In my last year, the program set records for conference (13) and total (24) wins and was nationally ranked for twenty-five weeks, compared to only eight weeks in its entire previous history, and the team's twenty-plus wins for the fifth straight season matched its number of twenty-win seasons in the previous forty-four years of the program.

* * *

Legendary IU basketball coach Bob Knight was fired on September 10, 2000, by then IU president Myles Brand, the mentor of my boss, IU President Michael McRobbie. As of my hiring almost a decade later—and continuing to the present day—passions about Coach Knight and his firing have run high throughout Hoosier Nation. For example, shortly after I became AD, a leading businessman offered to donate $1 million to IU Athletics if we would erect a statue of Coach Knight. He offered to make it $2 million if we added Myles Brand and made it a water feature "with Bob pissing on that son-of-a-bitch." I never told Michael about that one.

Regardless of your position on the continuum of opinions about Coach Knight and his firing, there can be no doubt that his estrangement from Indiana University basketball had been damaging to the program. All the other traditional blue-blood basketball programs in the country enjoy a strong connection with their patriarchs. John Wooden was a big part of UCLA his entire life. The foundational coaches at Kentucky (Adolph Rupp), North Carolina (Dean Smith), and Kansas (Phog Allen) all stayed closely involved with their universities, and each of their arenas are named after them. Mike Krzyzewski as of this writing is still the coach at Duke. Michigan State enjoys a direct connection to Jud Heathcote through current coach Tom Izzo, who was a Jud assistant. Not coincidentally, these schools enjoy very strong, broad support from their former players, which is often on full public display as they attend games.

Conversely, at Indiana, our greatest coach had made it clear to his former players, some of the most significant players in our history, that he considered it personally disloyal to him if they engaged with the IU basketball program. That presented those players with a very difficult choice of honoring their coach's wishes or enjoying a connection with the basketball program to which they had given, and been given, so much. While some of Coach Knight's most loyal players still came back on occasion, it is clear that the feud held the current program back. For that reason, I started gently and quietly to set the table for Coach Knight's literal and figurative return to IU basketball, knowing that the best I could do would be to remove obstacles for that to happen and to make sure he knew he was welcome. I suspected any kind of overt campaign would feel to Coach Knight as though we were trying to hotbox him and be counterproductive. I did not expect him to return quickly. I had significant doubts that he would return at all. I always believed if he did return, it would be because of his players and not anything I did or didn't do. I just wanted to make sure he and Hoosier Nation knew that he was welcome back.

Among the more significant overtures we made to Coach Knight was inducting him into the Indiana University Athletics Hall of Fame my first year as AD in 2009. He hadn't previously been inducted because of a well-intentioned, but in my view ultimately misguided, rule that living inductees had to be present at the induction. Since Coach Knight had always made clear that he wouldn't come, he had not been inducted. Regardless of how you feel about Coach Knight, I believed it was an embarrassment to our Hall of Fame that he wasn't in it given all he had accomplished for IU basketball. We rescinded the rule and inducted Coach Knight. He didn't attend but did provide a mostly positive letter, which was read at the ceremony. This was a very important first step in the healing process.

Later, when Coach Knight was in Indianapolis on his way to call a Purdue game for ESPN in West Lafayette, his longtime friend and the former Bloomington newspaper sportswriter Bob Hammel arranged for the three of us to have lunch at Rick's Boatyard Café at Eagle Creek, on the northwest side of Indianapolis. Lunch turned into a delightful five-hour visit, during which we discussed politics, history, sports, and current events but not a word about IU basketball. Coach Knight was relaxed, funny, and fascinating. He offered to be a sounding board for me on coaching searches in a variety of sports, again, without mentioning basketball. While it would be presumptuous and inaccurate to say that Coach Knight and I were ever friends, I think that meeting raised his comfort level with me. After that we corresponded a few times, mostly me inviting him to things and him declining those invitations. I also wrote him about the new sculptures in Simon Skjodt Assembly Hall, asking him if we could consider including him with the starting players and seniors from his undefeated 1976 national championship team. Under university rules, his permission was a prerequisite to being considered to be included. He wrote back declining, in classic Bob Knight fashion. I resigned to myself that he probably wouldn't be coming back, at least under my tenure, but I was comforted that we had done everything we could do to have tried to make that happen.

Then Randy Wittman from Coach Knight's 1980 Big Ten championship team invited him to the reunion we had planned for that team during our home game versus Purdue on Saturday, February 8, 2020, and he accepted! The sun, the moon, and the stars had finally aligned. Coach Knight had moved back to Bloomington. In fact, he and Bob Hammel had taken in an IU baseball game the previous spring, an important step, but not meant or seen as a reconciliation. His wife and son Pat were encouraging reconciliation. Coach had mellowed a bit, and time had done some of its thing on the wounds. Maybe his health challenges had made coming back more urgent for him. An invitation from Randy Wittman was a powerful one given his stature as one of Coach Knight's greatest and toughest players who went on to be a very well-respected NBA player and coach. Whatever the reason(s), Knight was planning to come back.

We were determined to keep this a player-driven and player-focused reunion and reconciliation. As you might imagine, there were a lot of people—other players, old friends, donors, fans, and the like—who wanted to be a part of the planning process. We established a very tight working group that made all the decisions surrounding the reunion. Randy Wittman and Quinn Buckner, probably the "dean" of the former Knight-era players and a then IU trustee, represented the former Knight players. Bob Hammel and longtime team physician Larry Rink, both close Knight friends, represented Coach Knight and his family. Deputy Athletic Director Scott Dolson, a former Knight manager and ultimately my successor as AD, represented the department. Randy and Quinn did a masterful job of keeping the event simple and focused on the players. The department invited every single Knight-era player, carefully defined by Randy and Quinn as any player who played for and/or was recruited by Coach Knight, including those who left early for the NBA, but not those who transferred to another school, to attend the player reunion. We never acknowledged in the invitation, however, that Coach Knight would be there because we just weren't sure, after all the years of declined invitations, that he would actually come this time. I had been the Charlie Brown to his Lucy enough times that I didn't want to proclaim publicly he was coming back only to have him decide not to come. Still, the former players, and increasingly the public, had heard he might attend the reunion game. In addition, Randy and Quinn led a separate players' effort to call Knight's former players to tell them Coach Knight was coming and to extend their personal request for them to attend.

It was decided that there would be a players-only gathering—with spouses and significant others, but no kids—with Coach Knight in Cook Hall, attached by tunnel to Simon Skjodt Assembly Hall, that would occur pregame. At halftime, each former player would be announced to the crowd before, hopefully, Coach Knight would be announced and, for the first time in more than twenty years, walk onto Branch McCracken Court. We offered to make special players-only jackets that Randy and Quinn designed with each player's name and number on them, which we gave to every former Knight player whether they attended or not. Quinn wanted to put the date of the reunion and a reference to Coach Knight's return on the jacket, but I was still concerned that Coach Knight might not come, which I felt would have turned the jackets from treasured mementos to embarrassing white elephants. I persuaded Quinn that a good alternative would be specially made, former-players-only Indiana basketball hats that said "Knight Time" with the date of the reunion. I instructed our staff not to hand out the hats until Coach Knight actually got there!

As you might imagine, everybody and their grandmother wanted to be in that gathering. Major IU Athletics donors. Former Knight colleagues. Important friends and/or extended family of players. Media personalities. University officials. But to their great credit, Randy and Quinn held strong and made no exceptions to the former-Knight-players-only guest list, even though it meant turning away some great IU friends and supporters. We set up Cook Hall with a comfortable feel of TVs, couches, tables and chairs, a buffet, and a bar. Coach sat on a couch, and one by one, or sometimes in small groups, the players—his players—would sit next to him to visit and reminisce. I also had the opportunity to shake his hand, welcome him back to Simon Skjodt Assembly Hall, and thank him for all that he had done for Indiana basketball.

During the game, I sat in my usual courtside seats with Barbara and our longtime close friends Mike and Patrice Schroeder, whom we had invited for moral support for this stressful day, along with my friends and IU alumni Mark Cuban and Sage Steele, as well as Sage's daughter, whom we were working to recruit to IU. Mark and Sage had expressed interest in being there for the momentous event. I guess I had been so close to it I had lost track that it was indeed a momentous event. Until it happened, I didn't even realize how grateful I was that it was happening. People were emotional. Many were crying. In part I think this was a result of the simple, player-driven nature of the ceremony, where each former player was introduced and walked across the floor. Many of them hadn't been back since their last game as a player. Then, finally, Coach Knight himself was introduced, through a tribute video the department's Cuban Center had produced, to a thundering standing ovation, and he walked to midcourt. The crowd was loving him, and Coach Knight was basking in their affection. As much as I had wanted this moment for Hoosier Nation, I had also wanted it for Coach. He deserved to have it.

Just about then, Mark leaned over to me and said, "Congratulations, Fred. You pulled it off, and it could not have gone better."

It was a very nice sentiment, and I graciously responded, "Shut the hell up! Don't jinx it. I'll celebrate when he's off the floor!" As if on cue, Coach Knight, egged on by the adoring crowd, started freelancing by exhorting the crowd to chant "defense," instructing former players to get into defensive stances, and trying to pull the headgear off ESPN's Dick Vitale, who was calling the game.

"I see what you mean," Mark said to me.

But all ended well. Pat Knight walked with his dad off the court, and with a final wave, he was gone. And in that instant, it seemed that twenty years of bile and separation were washed away by reconciliation and acceptance. The family was reunited. No longer would players have to choose between their coach and their school. It was a great moment for Hoosier Nation, Coach Knight and his players, and—by extension—the current Indiana University basketball program.

# 17. A FINAL WORD

Perhaps the very best of many wonderful things about being the athletic director at Indiana University was the opportunity to share it with my family. Indiana University is indeed a Glass family affair. Mom graduated from IU and started my love for the place from as early as I can remember. Barbara and I met at an IU football game and have three IU degrees between us. Daughter Katie and her husband, Tom, are alumni and also met at IU. Son Joe has an IU law degree and married an IU alumna, Emily. Sons Connor and George graduated from IU.

My first day as IU AD was Thursday, January 1, 2009, and the next day, Joe and I flew on a chartered jet with the men's basketball team for its game against Iowa in Carver-Hawkeye Arena. Within the next month, I also took George to Illinois, Katie to Northwestern, and Connor to Michigan State. What a treat it was to have this special time with each of my children so early in my tenure, setting the tone for the future. I wouldn't trade for anything the games, tailgates, trips, and the like with them and the rest of our family, which grew while I was AD to include not only Tom and Emily but also our grandchildren Betsy, Ellie, Anna Rose, and Lucy. Eli wasn't born until January 2020, so with the onset of the pandemic, he didn't get to partake in IU Athletics while I was AD. But as with his sister and cousins, I'm sure we'll be making lots of games after my return to civilian life. It wasn't something I expected or planned, but rooting on the Hoosiers together, home and away, live and on TV, with the special connection of being the AD was a special joy.

As we always have been, Barbara and I were a team closely following all the games, home and away, and enthusiastically participating in the department's events. We were a courtside staple at all the home men's basketball games and attended many of the women's as well.

A great memory is having all my granddaughters there for the WNIT championship game and storming the court with them when we won. In 2015, our whole then family went to the Maui Classic, and it was a special treat to travel with family to many of our football bowl games and tournament games in men's and women's basketball and men's soccer, among others. I could get very stressed out at games, but when I had one of my granddaughters on my lap, it lowered my blood pressure and kept the game in perspective. I was a nervous wreck at my last Crossroads Classic game in 2019, a nip and tuck affair against Notre Dame, until I held my granddaughter Anna Rose for the entire second half, which made me eerily calm, even as the thrilling last second shot gave us the win! I also remember taking Katie and two-year-old Betsy to Des Moines, Iowa, where we watched IU lose a tough NCAA tournament game to Wichita State. Just having Betsy there, with her innocent sense of wonder and sweetness, helped me keep that loss from wiping me out.

* * *

When I became AD in 2009 at age forty-nine, I believed that would be the last job I'd want to have and that I'd probably do it until sixty-five, or preferably seventy if I could get past the then mandatory sixty-five retirement age. But after the toll of separating from both of our power coaches, Kevin Wilson and Tom Crean, and hiring their replacements within one hundred days, by the summer of 2017, I started being open to the possibility of retiring from IU earlier than I had originally planned. As time continued to move on, although I still loved the job, I could feel it starting to take more out of me. Done right, it's an all-in, all-consuming responsibility, which is a big part of why I loved it; but it's also why I was feeling I couldn't keep doing it on an open-ended basis.

The Indiana University Bicentennial Year was coming up in 2019–2020. It was a very big deal for the university. In fact, we had been using it as an effective hook with both donors and the administration to get some major things accomplished "in time for the Bicentennial," particularly with regard to fundraising and facilities. We were forecasting that by the end of the Bicentennial we would not only exceed our very aggressive, unprecedented $215 million Bicentennial Capital Campaign goal, but we would also complete our Bicentennial Facilities Master Plan, which would cap off an investment of nearly a third of a billion dollars in much-needed facility projects.

I increasingly started to believe that it made sense to have the Bicentennial Year be my last year as AD. It was a logical bookend to my tenure with the completion of the Bicentennial Capital Campaign and Bicentennial Facilities Master Plan. By the end of the Bicentennial Year, I would have been AD for nearly twelve years, which would be three terms if I were working for an elected official (which is usually one term too long). Evan was ready to be done after his term-limited two terms as governor and again after two six-year terms in the Senate, and Bart was, reluctantly, I think, willing to do three, but the voters declined his invitation. The games—specifically men's basketball and football—were taking more and more out of me (and Barbara). They were less fun and more draining.

I also liked the idea of being able to go out on my own terms. At the time of the Bicentennial Year, seventeen Big Ten athletic directors had left those roles during my tenure as the AD at IU, and by my count, only two had done so on their own terms. The others had been fired or otherwise forced out either because they had made a mistake(s) or took the hit for broader culpability by their students, staff, and/or university. I knew going in these were tough jobs. Before I accepted the offer to be IU's AD, I told Barbara that the odds were that I would get fired for one of the reasons just described. I told her that I shouldn't take the job if we both couldn't be comfortable with that. To her great credit, she was. Accepting that was greatly emancipating for me. I had already absorbed and digested that possibility, which took away any fear of it. In fact, I specifically rejected having a term contract with IU, unlike probably every other AD in the country, because I wanted to make it clear I was betting on myself. It also had the benefit of aligning me more as a university vice president, all of whom also simply serve at the pleasure of the president. I never made any decision for the purpose of protecting my job. Sometimes the right thing to do is the thing that most puts your job at risk, and I was fine with that because I just wasn't worried about being fired. I much more cared about looking into the mirror and the faces of my wife and children knowing that I had done the right things as best as I could determine. If I did the right thing, then I could accept whatever criticism came with doing so. Always do the right thing, even when no one knows or appreciates that you are and even when the right thing looks to some like the wrong thing.

As the Bicentennial Year dawned in the summer of 2019, I had pretty much decided that it would be my last as AD. It was just time. I still loved it, but I was ready to step back and do something that kept me closer to home with more time with my grandchildren and the rest of my family. I didn't tell anyone but Barbara and, over time, my kids. A big driver for me was that I now had four grandchildren with a fifth on the way—all in Indianapolis—and I realized that I just wasn't going to be able to be a part of their lives the way I wanted to be with the demands of being IU's AD in Bloomington and traveling. I had done my best to be there for my kids when they were little, and I wanted to be there for my grandkids. I wanted to host sleepovers for them or take them out to breakfast on weekends instead of being on the road with the football or basketball team or in Bloomington attending one game or another. I wanted their parents to be able to call me to pick up a sick kid because I'd be ten minutes away in Indianapolis, not an hour and a half away in Bloomington. I wanted to be around to babysit them while their parents took a night off. So even though retiring would mean I'd lose some of the special time I had shared IU Athletics with my family, I was happy with the trade-off of being able to be more generally present and a part of their lives.

At first, I thought I would "retire, retire," but as I tried that on, Ignatian style, it never felt good to me. I realized that I had more in the tank and that it was too early to go to just not working, even with a healthy dose of volunteer work and family time. For me, the right balance at this stage of my life, having recently turned sixty, seemed to be returning full-time to Indianapolis, affiliating with a large law firm there, robustly returning to the practice of law, and—freed from the extraordinary demands and scrutiny of being the AD—having lots of time to be a part of the lives of my grandchildren. Without hardly anyone else knowing, I started living the last year's calendar knowing that it was my last all-staff meeting report, Hall of Fame Dinner, home football game, and the like. It was reaffirming to me that those didn't make me sad but rather excited for whatever would be coming next. As with leaving previous big jobs, like with Evan and Bart, it was made easier for me because I had followed the advice to take my job seriously, not myself. Being AD was what I did, not who I was. It was simply another steward's turn.

Even before the season, I had intended to extend Tom Allen's contract after the 2019 football season, and given its historic success, that only became clearer as the season moved to its conclusion. I had also always intended to tell him as part of our postseason contract conversations of my impending departure, but the need to do so only became more significant when he asked me straight out about my future plans. Because I hadn't yet told the president, I told Tom I wasn't in a position to respond, but he deserved that answer, and I would give it to him as soon as I could. I also emphasized that he was signing a contract with Indiana University, not Fred Glass, and if the president and trustees stepped up to endorse the kind of contract we were discussing, it should give him great comfort.

I called the president that same day (December 4) and asked to meet with him right away to update him on the contract negotiations. We met that night in his office. I told him of my retirement plans and why I felt I needed to tell him now, before I told Tom, which I needed to do soon. I also told him I wanted to make it public very soon. My experience was that such secrets don't keep very well, and I didn't want some unexpected, interceding event to occur that might be pointed to as the "real" reason I was retiring. Michael understandably wanted more time to digest this unexpected turn of events and discuss it with the board of trustees, so we waited several days before making the announcement. To my pleasant surprise, the news didn't leak out before we publicly announced it on December 16. I was gratified by President McRobbie's statement upon the announcement of my retirement:

> I want to congratulate Fred Glass on behalf of Indiana University and personally, on a superb tenure as Indiana University's Vice President and Director of Intercollegiate Athletics. He has done an outstanding job in all areas of his portfolio and IU is seeing levels of accomplishment academically and athletically by its student athletes that rank with the best it has ever achieved. His legacy will be one of strong and competitive athletics programs and teams that play by the rules, and pervasive commitment to compliance and integrity, a commitment to excellent academic performance, record fund-raising and magnificent new or renovated facilities. He is also widely respected as one of the best athletics directors in the Big Ten and has represented IU nationally with the greatest distinction. I wish him the very best in the next phase of his career, already filled with many notable achievements.

So as I sat there on December 16, I looked forward to enjoying finishing out my final season as AD going to basketball tournament games, watching softball and baseball games, and the like, hopefully with continuing strong performances. Yes, it was shaping up to be a great year, and then March 11 happened.

It was Wednesday night, the first of the Big Ten men's basketball tournament, and I was with Barbara and our daughter Katie at Bankers Life Fieldhouse watching IU beat Nebraska to almost assuredly clinch an invitation to the NCAA tournament. Of course, we knew of COVID-19 and were tracking developments (just the day before, I had established the IU Athletics Medical Advisory Group to provide expert medical advice to me and the department regarding COVID-19), but things still seemed relatively normal. March 11 was the last day of normal. The day had started with all the Big Ten ADs, Big Ten staff, and many others meeting together in a relatively small room in Bankers Life Fieldhouse. There were handshakes, hugs, and open common bowls of pretzels and potato chips. Before the game, we had gone out to a nice dinner across from the arena in a restaurant crowded with basketball fans and others. At the game, we all sat close together with other IU fans, cheering and talking. And then it started to change.

First we could see that Nebraska's coach was obviously very ill with what appeared to be flu-like symptoms, but he continued to coach. Big Ten Network analyst Andy Katz told Archie before the game "to stay away from [Fred] Hoiberg because there is something wrong with him." It was later diagnosed as "just" the flu, which begs the question of why he was coaching even if he thought it was just the flu. Then we saw on our phones that the NBA Utah Jazz's Rudy Gobert had tested positive for COVID-19, leading to their game against the Oklahoma City Thunder being postponed shortly before tipoff. At the time, this was a shocking development.

Of course, then the dominos started to fall. The Big Ten canceled its tournament, and the other conferences did the same. The NCAA tournament was ultimately canceled, and all the major professional sports leagues ultimately postponed their seasons. COVID-19 consumed not only sports but the nation and the world. I went in the following Monday, March 16, to meet with my head coaches and senior staff. That was my last day in the office. The final three and a half months of my term as AD were spent on endless telephone and Zoom calls dealing with the scourge of COVID-19 and later also the scourge of racism.

On May 25, 2020, African American George Floyd was killed in Minneapolis by a White police officer who knelt on Floyd's neck while he was handcuffed, lying face down, begging for his life, and saying, "I can't breathe." Like most thinking Americans, our students and staff were devastated and outraged over this senseless and inexcusable killing. Protests sprung up all around the country and continued at one level or another through the balance of my tenure as AD.

Shortly after the Floyd killing, I convened a Zoom meeting of the students comprising the Athletic Director's Council on Diversity and Inclusivity, which I had formed in 2016 in response to the racist, homophobic, and anti-immigrant rhetoric of that presidential campaign and been meeting with monthly since that time. That we all knew each other helped lead to a very open, emotional, powerful, and productive conversation. Afterward, I made a rather extensive public statement denouncing Floyd's killing, reinforcing that we love our students, recognizing they are hurting, and declaring, "We can't let ourselves be content to send the Floyd family our 'thoughts and prayers' and then lapse into moving on to other things, or we will be condemning ourselves to continuing to endure these kind of atrocities, and George Floyd's death will have been in vain." We built upon our Zoom call with the council to have similar separate calls with our head coaches, department staff, and students, during which I heard raw, powerful, and moving testimony about the impact of racism on our people in their daily lives. Although I had always known intellectually that as a White person, I was inherently privileged, hearing directly from our African American students and colleagues their personal experiences with racism seared it into me emotionally. I thought I knew. I didn't know.

As a first step, the magis, in translating our conversations into action, we established mandatory, in-person inclusivity training for all staff and students; a major new Excellence Academy program on civics, citizenship, and voter education for students; Election Day as a mandatory day off for students from all athletically related activities; the Indiana University Athletics Anti-Hate and Anti-Racism Coalition; that the Athletic Director's Council on Diversity and Inclusivity would continue under my successor; and staff-wide and student-wide conversations at least once every semester on issues relating to race. As I said in my communication to all staff and students just a week after the first meeting with the council, "While almost any action seems insufficient given the overwhelming challenge that racism poses to all of us, that can't deter us into inaction. We need to be the change we want to see in the world. This first round of action items is a good start, but it's just a start. We will stay committed, engaged, and active in fighting racism and securing racial justice and equality."

Among all the bad and often tragic news, there had been some good news. On March 17, 2020, President McRobbie announced that he had appointed Deputy Athletic Director Scott Dolson to be my successor as vice president and director of intercollegiate athletics. I was thrilled. Even more so than being happy for my friend who had been an extraordinarily effective second-in-command for virtually my entire tenure as AD, I was happy for the department because I knew what a tremendous leader Scott would be. I confess that it was also gratifying to have my time as AD endorsed by the president and the board of trustees by having my deputy and proposed successor selected to be the next IU AD.

Although we conducted a very collaborative, collegial, and successful transition, it became a challenging one as a result of COVID-19 and the social unrest set off by the George Floyd killing and years and years of systemic racism. I made clear to Scott from the beginning that, as with other positions I had departed, I would accept the responsibility to "be the AD until I'm not" and run through the tape—but then I would exit the stage completely so as not to be underfoot when Scott officially and completely took the reins on July 1, 2020. And that's how we did it. On my last day, I sent a memo to all students about returning to campus in light of COVID-19, which, among other things, made clear that if they did not want to participate in athletics because of COVID-19 concerns, IU Athletics would continue to honor their scholarships. After my last Zoom call on my last day, with our head coaches, I got in the car with Barbara and drove to Michigan to start my retirement from IU. Other than happily and completely engaging in any calls for counsel from Scott, I have stayed out of his way. When you go out, go out the right way.

* * *

I am grateful for the opportunity I had to come back to my alma mater to heal and lead IU Athletics. We followed the rules. We graduated our students at a record rate. Competitively, most of our programs were doing historically well, and the futures seem bright for all our sports. Our department was recognized for being extraordinarily well managed fiscally. We were an athletic department nationally known for the holistic care and development of our students. We had unprecedented success with fundraising and facility development. I had returned to Indiana University to rebuild the foundation of an athletic department that needed rebuilding, culturally and physically, and I was leaving proud that we had accomplished just that.

* * *

As my retirement date from IU drew closer, I was often asked what I thought my legacy would be. My belief is that for better or worse, we do not get to write our own legacies. That certainly applies to my time at IU, as well as in government, the law, politics, and my other communities and with my friends and even my family. Rather, our legacies live in the hearts and minds of the people we have touched. I hope those folks have good feelings about me.

My daughter Katie planted the seed of this book with her Father's Day gift to me in 2018: a year-long email subscription asking me to answer weekly questions about my life. If I were to receive one of those emails today and it were to ask, "What have you learned?" I might respond, "Life is not a dress rehearsal. It's the real thing and our only shot. So don't put off seizing opportunities because you feel you aren't ready, or capable, or deserving, but rather take ownership of them by believing in yourself and making your own luck."

I did it, Mom.

# REFERENCES

Alesia, Mark. 2008. "Indiana Gets 3 Years' Probation." *Indianapolis Star*, November 26, 2008.

Associated Press. 1993. "Casino Companies Court Democrats." *Indianapolis Star*, August 20, 1993.

Bailey, F. Lee. 1971. *The Defense Never Rests*. New York: Stein and Day.

Ballard, Greg. 2005. *The Ballard Rules: Small Unit Leadership*. Bloomington, IN: Author-House.

Branch, Taylor. 2011. "The Shame of College Sports." *Atlantic*, October 2011.

Capshew, James. 2012. *Herman B Wells: The Promise of the American University*. Bloomington: Indiana University Press.

Davis, Andrea. 2007. "Too Close to Quit? City Gained Momentum with Super Bowl Bid; New Try Likely." *Indianapolis Business Journal*, May 28, 2007.

Eschbacher, Karen. 2007. "Bowl-Bid Loss Puts Indy in Rare Air." *Indianapolis Star*, May 29, 2007.

Glass, Fred. 2004. "The Best Way to Fund the Stadium Deal." *Indianapolis Star*, December 26, 2004.

Hammel, Bob. 2008. *The Bill Cook Story: Ready, Fire, Aim!* Bloomington: Indiana University Press.

Hanley, Marge. 1978. "Tavern Has Roots in Pub." *Indianapolis News*, June 15, 1978.

Kennedy, Sheila. 2009. "The Hunt for Blue November." *Indianapolis Star*, May 11, 2009.

Ketzenberger, John. 2007. "Maurer Knows That a Great Opportunity Blew on By." *Indianapolis Star*, April 3, 2007.

———. 2008. "Vision Helped Super Tuesday Become a Reality." *Indianapolis Star*, May 21, 2008.

King, Stephen. 2000. *On Writing: A Memoir of the Craft*. New York: Simon & Shuster.

Lamott, Anne. 1995. *Bird by Bird: Some Instructions on Writing and Life*. New York: Anchor Books.

Lee, Harper. 1960. *To Kill a Mockingbird*. Philadelphia: J. B. Lippincott.

Lenoir, Lisa. 1989. "Physical Fitness Is Net Result of Addition to Bayh's Home." *Indianapolis Star*, June 4, 1989.

*Madison Weekly Herald*. 1876. November 16, 1876.

———. 1878. February 13, 1878.

———. 1878. July 10, 1878.

———. 1879. September 24, 1879.

———. 1880. November 10, 1880.

———. 1881. "The End of the Farce." May 4, 1881.

———. 1881. "Gordon Accomplished His Work and Got His Pay." May 4, 1881.

Martin, James. 2010. *The Jesuit Guide to (Almost) Everything: A Spirituality for Real Life*. New York: HarperCollins.

Olmsted, Larry. 2012. "Super Bowl XLVI's Real Winner? Indianapolis!" *Forbes*, February 6, 2012.

O'Shaughnessy, Brendan. 2007. "Mayor: Let's Try for the 2012 Game." *Indianapolis Star*, May 24, 2007.

Osterman, Zach. 2019. "Glass: IU 'Program Is Going in the Right Direction' under Allen." *Indianapolis Star*, October 28, 2019.

———. 2019. "'No Apologies': Indiana Basketball Might Not Be Back among Nation's Elite, but It Sure Spends Like It." *Indianapolis Star*, August 20, 2019.

Ruthhart, Bill. 2007. "Peterson Appointee to Leave City Post." *Indianapolis Star*, November 13, 2007.

Schneider, Mary Beth, and Matthew Tully. 2005. "Governor Says Colts Stadium Deal in Doubt." *Indianapolis Star*, April 29, 2005.

Snider, Mike. 2000. "Pop Up Bill Clinton Fundraising Videos." *Mad Magazine*, November 2000.

Tobias, Randy. 2003. *Put the Moose on the Table: Lessons in Leadership from a CEO's Journey through Business and Life*. Bloomington: Indiana University Press.

Tully, Matthew. 2005. "Stadium's Fate Unclear as Clock Winds Down." *Indianapolis Star*, April 27, 2005.

———. 2005 "Stadium Wins, 108–36." *Indianapolis Star*, April 30, 2005.

———. 2008. "Super Bowl Victory Cry: 'Got It!'" *Indianapolis Star*, May 21, 2008.

Wells, Herman B. 1980. *Being Lucky: Reminiscences and Reflections*. Bloomington: Indiana University Press.

Woititz, Janet Geringer. 1983. *Adult Children of Alcoholics*. Deerfield Beach, FL: Health Communications, Inc.

# INDEX